WE
WORSHIP

To Carol and Paul,
Mary Etta and Mike,
Gail and Frank,
Kathy and Den—
twenty-five years, and counting,
of study and sharing

OTHER BOOKS
BY FATHER LUKEFAHR

We Live
To Know, Love, and Serve God

We Pray
Living in God's Presence

The Search for Happiness
Four Levels of Emotional and Spiritual Growth

"We Believe..."
A Survey of the Catholic Church

Christ's Mother and Ours
A Catholic Guide to Mary

The Catechism Handbook

The Privilege of Being Catholic

A Catholic Guide to the Bible

WE
WORSHIP
A GUIDE TO THE
CATHOLIC MASS

Newly Updated With
the *Roman Missal*,
Third Edition

Oscar Lukefahr, CM

Liguori
LIGUORI, MISSOURI

Imprimi Potest: Richard Thibodeau, C.Ss.R., Provincial
Denver Province, The Redemptorists

Imprimatur: Most Reverend Robert J. Hermann, V.G.
Auxiliary Bishop of St. Louis

Published by Liguori Publications, Liguori, Missouri; liguori.org

Library of Congress Cataloging-in-Publication Data
Lukefahr, Oscar.
   We worship : a guide to the Catholic Mass / Oscar Lukefahr.—1st ed.
     p.   cm.
   Includes bibliographical references.
   ISBN 978-0-7648-1212-5
   1. Mass. 2. Catholic Church—Liturgy. I. Title.

BX2230.3.L85 2004
264'.02—dc22   2004048740

Liguori Publications, a nonprofit corporation, is an apostolate of the Redemptorists (redemptorists.com).

Printed in the United States of America
14 13 12 11 / 10 9 8 7

CONTENTS

"In his Apostolic Letter, *Novo Millennio Ineunte*, 'At the Close of the Great Jubilee of the Year 2000,' our Holy Father Pope John Paul II sets forth the pastoral program for the Church at the beginning of the Third Christian Millennium. The new millennium, a time which is marked by a thoroughgoing secularism, a pervasive forgetfulness of God, requires, as the Holy Father has repeatedly reminded us, that the Church carry out a new evangelization, the teaching and living of the faith with the enthusiasm and energy of the first Christians....

"For the work of the new evangelization, our Holy Father has wanted to stir up anew with us wonder and awe before the great gift and mystery of the Holy Eucharist. To use his words, he has wanted 'to rekindle this Eucharistic amazement' (*Ecclesia de Eucharistia*, n. 6). To grow in the likeness of Christ, we must contemplate His face through prayers and through the many ways in which He makes Himself known to us in the Church....

"*We Worship: A Guide to the Catholic Mass* provides an excellent help in rekindling 'Eucharistic amazement' within us. It also provides a solid introduction to the mystery of the Holy Eucharist for those who are coming to the faith....

"May your reading and study of *We Worship: A Guide to the Catholic Mass* help you to grow in 'Eucharistic amazement,' in wonder and awe at the gift and mystery of the Holy Eucharist. ...Through the intercession of the Blessed Virgin Mary, 'Woman of the Eucharist,' may we all grow in holiness of life through Eucharistic faith and devotion."

MOST REVEREND RAYMOND L. BURKE
JULY 2004

FOREWORD

⌒〜⌇〜〜

She was young, beautiful, a prominent socialite from a prestigious family, a patriot during the Revolutionary War, the mother of five children, a devout Episcopalian, a woman of charm and education—and now, a widow. Her beloved husband, William, had succumbed to tuberculosis on a business cruise with his wife to Livorno, Italy, in 1803. While there for some months to tend to the burial of William, grieve, and to wait for a ship to bring her back home to New York, she was given hospitality by business acquaintances of her late husband, the Fillichi family. In her grief, she rediscovered a genuine religious hunger for a deeper relationship with God, and was very moved by the faith and devotion of her hosts, especially by their love for Jesus in the Eucharist. She would often accompany them to Mass; she would marvel as they prepared for holy Communion, and was in awe of their reverence. On early evening walks she would make visits to the Blessed Sacrament with them, and kneel with simple, childlike trust before the tabernacle.

Then it happened. It was the Feast of Corpus Christi, and she went with the family to stand on the corner while the procession with the Eucharist passed by. As all the Italians knelt down in quiet prayer and adoration, she, shyly at the back of the crowd, heard another American snidely remark, "These peasants think that bread is really the Son of God!" Deep in her soul, the answer came forth, "So do I!" When she returned to New York, she began instructions in the Catholic faith and, at the cost of much sacrifice, scorn, loss of family, friends, and wealth, she entered the Church in 1805.

What's more, on September 14, 1975, Pope Paul VI canonized her as the first native-born American saint. Her name? Elizabeth Ann Bayley Seton.

That's the awesome power of the Eucharist, my friends. That's the draw, the magnetism, of the Blessed Sacrament.

The Eucharist is "the mystery of faith" which we can never fully comprehend. But that does not mean we should not study this mystery, read about it, meditate on it, and pray often before it and about it.

I am here to introduce you to an excellent tool to help us appreciate this sacred mystery all the more. I have been a fan of Father Oscar Lukefahr, C.M., for years, and have come to appreciate very much his lucid, succinct, and effective books and lessons on our Catholic faith. This is one of his best yet. And how providential that it comes out as we begin the "Year of the Eucharist" proclaimed by Pope John Paul II.

All over today we detect a "hunger" within our people, not unlike that experienced by Saint Elizabeth Ann Seton. Commentators tell us about a rising interest in "spirituality." Remember what Pope Saint Pius X taught: "This side of paradise, there is no better way to be united to Jesus than by worthily receiving Him in Holy Communion."

O Sacrament Most Holy,
O Sacrament Divine,
All praise and all thanksgiving,
Be every moment thine!

Let us proclaim this mystery of faith!

MOST REVEREND TIMOTHY M. DOLAN
JULY 2004

ACKNOWLEDGMENTS

S incere thanks to all who helped in the writing of *We Worship: A Guide to the Catholic Mass*...to Cecelia Portlock, who oversaw this project, for invaluable advice and cheerful assistance; to Judy Bauer, who suggested the project; to Evelyn John, who designed the interior; to Wendy Barnes for the beautiful cover; to Pam Hummelsheim and Maureen Connolly for editorial help on the 2011 update and to Penny Elder for proofreading it; to Paul and Carol Berens, Mike and Mary Etta Dunaway, Frank and Gail Jones, and Den and Kathy Vollink, who discussed each chapter at our monthly study group meetings; to the religious-education class of Saint Vincent de Paul Parish in Perryville, Missouri, whose enthusiasm, suggestions, comments, and proofreading made every chapter better; to Sister Delores Schilli, who organized and made arrangements for the class; to Father Charles Shelby, C.M., for ideas and advice; to Father John Gagnepain, C.M., whose encouragement helped get this book from concept to reality; to Rob Hurley and Dan Triller for ideas and encouragement; to the Saint Benedict Monday Morning "Play Group" of Broken Arrow, Oklahoma, for their lively support, comments, and suggestions. I am grateful to Most Reverend Raymond L. Burke, for reading the original manuscript, for helpful suggestions, and for his positive comments. Finally, I want to express special thanks to the Most Reverend Timothy M. Dolan for enthusiastic support and for writing the Foreword. May God bless you all!

INTRODUCTION:
PEOPLE OF FAITH

⁓✦⁓

"Mass Confusion"

A few years ago, Sunday morning found four families in a southeastern Missouri town doing their best to keep holy the Lord's Day. As Frank and Gail hurried to get their three children ready for Mass, they met resistance from three-year-old Meghan, who couldn't find her patent leather shoes—or anything else. "I want my doll," she wailed, "and my blanket and pillow!" The family got to the church on time, but when Mass began, Ryan and Natalie busied themselves trying to push each other out of the pew—and their parents' concentration out the window.

Mike and Mary Etta were having their own problems preparing for Mass. From upstairs came a thunderous crash. Their two-year-old son had knocked over a full-length mirror, and broken glass was shining brightly over most of the hallway floor.

Paul and Carol, driving to Mass with their three boys, asked if anyone had given the dog his heart pill. Christian shook his head no. Tyler said, "I did." "Me too," chimed in Josh. At Mass, the parents found their efforts at devotion besieged by fears that little Pepé, with his overdose of heart medication, might be teetering on the fine line between this world and a doggie cemetery.

Den and Kathy and their two boys made it to church without incident, and participated in the liturgy with devotion. But during the Lord's Prayer, devotion began to slip away. Tim and Matt seemed more interested in pinching each other and creating new trespasses rather than forgiving old ones.

KEEP HOLY THE LORD'S DAY

Why would parents put up with lost shoes, broken mirrors, doggie drug overdoses, and mischievous children to attend Mass? Why, for that matter, would the first Christians brave threats of Roman swords and hungry lions to gather for the Eucharist? Why would twentieth-century believers ignore threats of torture and death to celebrate Mass secretly in a communist gulag?

Because more than two thousand years ago a newborn baby's cry broke the night's stillness at Bethlehem. Because thirty-three years later he died on a cross as onlookers heard another cry, "Father, into your hands I commend my spirit." Because on the third day after his crucifixion, that same man appeared, risen and glorious, to his followers. Because that man is, incredibly, the God who created the universe, the God who sustains us in being, and the God before whom all human beings must stand at the moment of death. Because that Man-God is the only one who can bring us through that moment to the fullness of life eternal. Because the Mass unites believers of every age to the birth, life, death, and Resurrection of that Man-God, our Lord and Savior, Jesus Christ.

Can an hour at Mass actually connect us to Jesus Christ and to the power of his life, death, and Resurrection? You have his word on it! It is the purpose of this book to study this word, to explore the meaning and power of the Mass.

In Chapter One we will answer the question: "Why go to Mass?" In Chapter Two we will survey the fascinating history of the Mass. We will note its roots in the Old Testament and its institution in the New. We will see how the Mass evolved through the centuries into the celebration we know today. Chapter Three will walk us through the Mass, step by step, explaining its environment, words, and actions, including those revisions mandated in the new *General Instruction of the Roman Missal* (Washington, D.C.: United States Catholic Conference, Inc., 2003). Chapter Four will explore ways of participating that can open us to the full significance and efficacy of the Mass. Chapter Five will focus on holy Communion and its meaning. Chapter Six answers frequently asked questions about the Mass. Chapter Seven will conclude the book with suggestions for a Catholic spirituality built on the foundation of the Eucharist.

SPIRITUAL VISION

Before we embark on this journey of exploration and discovery, we must pray for the wisdom and enlightenment that only God can give. Just as physical vision can be clouded so gradually by cataracts that people don't realize how faulty their sight has become, so can our spiritual vision be clouded by routine, distraction, and weariness, or obscured when the light of faith grows dim. Several years ago I had cataract surgery and was amazed to discover how my vision had improved. "Doctor Kies," I remarked to the physician who had performed the operations, "Did you know there are big green signs on interstate highways that tell you where the cities are?" He just sighed.

The Mass presents signposts on life's pathway that are far more important than any road markers. But we need eyes of faith that are trained to see spiritual realities. Den was holding his daughter, aged two, at Mass and she was a bit restless. As the priest lifted up the host just before holy Communion, Den directed his daughter's gaze toward the altar. "Look, Mary Beth," he said,

"That's Jesus the priest is holding." Mary Beth looked intently at the priest, then replied, "That's not Jesus. That's bread." Then she turned to her dad, pinched his cheek, and asked, "Daddy, do you need glasses?"

That was many years ago, and Daddy didn't need glasses. But Mary Beth needed eyes of faith to see Jesus under the sign of bread. As a two-year-old, she couldn't be expected to have such vision. But now that she has received her first holy Communion, she does see Jesus at Mass, and she knows Daddy was right. The priest *was* holding Jesus.

I pray that this book will help all of us see Jesus more clearly at every Mass. Let's pray that Jesus, who opened the eyes of the physically blind, will open the eyes of our souls to see the glory that surrounds every celebration of the Eucharist. As you read this book, and as you participate in the Eucharist, may the Lord be with you!

FR. OSCAR LUKEFAHR, C.M.

TERMINOLOGY

A word about the word *Mass* and other words referring to this sacred action. Jesus celebrated the first Mass at a Jewish Passover celebration, his "Last Supper" before his death and Resurrection. So in the New Testament the Mass is called the *Lord's Supper* (1 Cor 11:20) and the *breaking of the bread*, because at the Last Supper Jesus took a loaf of bread and broke it before changing it into his own body (Lk 22:19; Acts 2:42; 20:7). Because of its origin in a Passover meal, the Mass is called the *Paschal Meal*, from *pesah*, the Jewish word for Passover. The Mass is called the *Eucharist*, a word coming from the Greek word for thanksgiving, an essential part of the Jewish Passover rite and the prayer of Jesus at the Last Supper (1 Cor 11:24). The term *Mass* began to be used only in the fourth century. It originated in the words used for dismissing people at the end of the ceremony, *Ite, missa est* (Go, the Mass is ended); this *missio,* or sending forth, implies that the Mass is to be brought into our everyday lives. The Mass is called the *Divine Liturgy; liturgy* came from a Greek word meaning a work on behalf of people. *Liturgy* is used in the Church not only in regard to the entire Mass, but also to parts of the Mass (Liturgy of the Word and Liturgy of the Eucharist), and to the other sacraments and acts of worship.

These terms, and others, are explained in detail in the *Catechism of the Catholic Church,* paragraphs 1328–1332 and 1347. (References to the *Catechism* will henceforth be given as *CCC,* followed by paragraph numbers.) Note also that in this book God's chosen people of the Old Covenant will be referred to as Hebrews, Israelites, Jews, or the Jewish people.

Chapter One

WHY GO TO MASS?

⌒─✦─⌐

Hugh, a resident of a veterans' home in southeastern Missouri, said that during World War II he often attended Mass celebrated on a makeshift altar, such as the hood of a jeep. On one occasion in a combat zone in the Philippines, Mass was being offered on a large block of wood when a Japanese Zero fighter roared overhead on a strafing run. Priest and soldiers huddled on the ground near the altar until the fighter disappeared. Then Mass resumed.

I asked Hugh why he attended Mass under such conditions. He replied, "I wanted to, and so did the other soldiers. We knew we needed God."

We need God too. But in the relative comfort and safety of our modern world, we can forget this. So we have to examine the reasons why we should attend Mass.

THE CONNECTION BETWEEN MASS AND LIFE

The first of these reasons is the manner in which Mass relates to the human condition. As we consider our humanity, we realize that we need food, clothing, and shelter. We want to relate to others, to love and be loved. We long to be happy.

As we try to meet such needs and desires, we face challenges and obstacles. Satisfying bodily appetites requires hard work. Getting along with others is difficult; friendships fade and families quarrel. Our own weaknesses and failures dishearten us. Crime, terrorism, and war cast dark shadows over humanity. Our desire for life is countered by the realization that we must die.

What is wrong? When and why did life go wrong? Can it be righted? Human beings have struggled with these questions for millennia. The Judeo-Christian tradition traces our problems back to the fact that humanity has misused the freedom granted by God at creation. The first man and woman, given freedom so they might love God and others and thus achieve true happiness, chose to reject God's designs. They cut themselves off from God and each other. Their sin affected their descendants, who sank deeper into every kind of malice and tragedy.

Humanity could not bridge the resulting void between itself and its Creator. So God reached out to us, establishing a point of contact through the Jewish people. Then God did the unimaginable. God, a loving community of Persons—Father, Son, and Holy Spirit—entered our world when the Son took on human nature as Jesus Christ. Jesus brought to humanity God's limitless love. Enemies, resenting his message that God loves all people, tried to silence him. But he persevered, even when he realized this would mean death. "No one has greater love than this, to lay down one's life for one's friends" (Jn 15:13). Jesus' death on a cross was the greatest act of love in history, a sacrifice that repaired the breach between God and us.

Since Jesus was God as well as human, death could not hold him and was conquered by his Resurrection. Jesus lives forever as Lord and Savior, joining us to himself in his Church, which continues his visible presence on earth. Jesus invites all to be one with him, to accept the power of divine love which can bring us through every trial, even death, to eternal happiness.

Here the Mass comes in. The death and Resurrection of Jesus

are not just historical events. They touch us today through the Eucharist. On the night before he died, Jesus gathered his apostles around a table where he took bread and said, "This is my body" (Mt 26:26). He took a cup of wine and said, "This is the cup of my blood. Do this in memory of me" (see Lk 22:19). The first Christians understood that these words united them to Christ's death and Resurrection. "For as often as you eat this bread and drink the cup," Paul writes, "you proclaim the Lord's death until he comes" (1 Cor 11:26).

God is not limited by space or time. God makes the saving power of Christ's death and Resurrection available to us at every Mass. At every Mass, we are sacramentally transported to the room where Jesus gives us the Eucharist, the hill where he dies, and the empty tomb where we meet the risen Christ.

If we truly realized the miracle that occurs at every Mass, we would take off our shoes, like Moses at the burning bush, and fall down in awe. At the least, we ought with joy and gratitude to enter the place where Mass is celebrated. Here God's love and grace wash over our lives to give meaning and hope. And at Mass we express in prayer and worship what we believe about God's greatness and about...

OUR PLACE IN GOD'S CREATION

Our home is planet Earth. It spins around the Sun, one of a hundred billion stars in the Milky Way galaxy. The Milky Way is one of many billions of galaxies, part of a universe so vast that if we could travel at the speed of light (186,282 miles per second), we'd need thirty billion years to traverse its current diameter. If the universe were reduced by a trillion, with our Sun the size of a grain of sand, our galaxy would be a beach 600,000 miles across, and the universe would still stretch to limits beyond imagining.

Our life span on planet Earth may last a hundred years. This seems a long time, but compared to the age of the universe, it shrinks into insignificance. To show how our lives fit into the pattern of time, astronomer Carl Sagan recommended that we compress the fifteen billion years our universe has existed into one calendar year. The universe began on January 1. Earth was formed on September 14. Dinosaurs appeared on Christmas Eve. Human beings began to exist on December 31 at 10:30 P.M. Jesus lived just four seconds ago. The longest human life is but one fifth of a second.

Either we are tiny specks on an insignificant planet whirling around a sun burning itself out in a tired galaxy lost in a vast universe;
or
we are children of God, who is powerful enough to create the universe with a word; wise enough to design it for fifteen billion years of ceaseless motion; and generous enough to grant us the priceless gifts of life, knowledge, and love.

Either we are wisps of chemicals held together by the glue of chance for a brief moment of life, existing without any underlying cause or meaning;
or
we are people created for a marvelous journey, destined to be ushered by death into a new life that will place us in the everlasting presence of God and blessed with the joy, peace, and security we long for.

Either there exists no one greater than ourselves; no ultimate reason for existence; no rescue from hatred, violence, and death, because we came from nothing and are doomed to return to nothing;

or

there exists a God whose Being is knowledge, love, and personality—Father, Son, and Holy Spirit—in whose image we are made. And the Son entered our space and time; took on humanity as Jesus Christ; died on a cross to conquer evil and death; rose from the grave to reign forever; and gave us a miracle allowing us to become one with him in his life, death, and Resurrection and through him to be united with the Father and Holy Spirit.

We who are Catholic stand with twenty centuries of believers in refusing to accept littleness, meaninglessness, nothingness. At Mass we stand with Christ to proclaim our belief in the presence of God, in the inevitable victory of love over hatred and of life over death. We treasure the miracle Jesus gave us, the miracle of the Eucharist.

TOUCHING GOD

We may suppose that going to Mass is an obligation imposed by the Church or a nice custom or the social thing to do. But Mass lies at the heart of our existence. It defines what we believe about God, about life and death, about right and wrong. We cannot attend Mass without imprinting something significant on our very being. We cannot carelessly miss Mass without affecting who we are, what we believe, and where we stand on life's most essential questions.

The size of the universe and the scope of time are so vast we cannot comprehend them. How much greater is the Being who created both time and space! If the universe God made is too much to grasp, how can we contact God in any realistic way? We can't, on our own. But God reaches out to us at a point where the universe stands still, the Mass. As we "condense" time and space to get some sense of their magnitude, so God "condenses" divinity in Jesus to reveal the incredible extent of divine love in the heart of God. Then Jesus "condenses" the power of his life, death, and Resurrection in the Mass; he "condenses" his humanity and divinity in the Eucharist. Through the Mass and in holy Communion, we meet God!

If we are to understand the reasons for going to Mass, we must consider what happens at the Eucharist, whom we receive at Communion, and how one hour can affect our lives. At Mass we touch the divine, we reach through the veil that separates time from eternity and grasp the hand of Jesus. We are drawn from the routine of everyday life to be "filled with all the fullness of God" (Eph 3:19).

REAL HAPPINESS

We want to be happy. God wants us to be happy. But happiness is elusive. There are various levels of happiness: satisfying bodily appetites, achieving worthwhile goals, helping others. But these are transient. Only the joy that comes from God will last forever. Unless we build our lives on the sure foundation of God's love, we will never achieve lasting happiness.

The Mass is essential to our search for happiness. Pope John Paul II writes in his apostolic letter *Dies Domini* that "we must rediscover this aspect of the life of faith....Sunday is the day of joy in a very special way, indeed the day most suitable for learning how to rejoice and to rediscover the true nature and deep roots of joy" (57; find this document at cin.org/jp2/diesdomi.html; accessed January 12, 2011).

I wonder how many of us come to the Eucharist on Sunday expecting to be filled with happiness. As I prepare for Mass, I'm sometimes concerned about problems that need resolving, friends who are facing difficulties, and global issues such as terrorism.

Weighed down by such worries, I'm not a very positive sign of hope, peace, or joy as I process to the altar.

But my problems are insignificant compared to those Christ endured on the night before he died. He awaited a terrible day of ghastly suffering, abandonment by his disciples, and shouldering an unimaginable burden, the sins of humankind. Nevertheless, he radiated peace and joy. "I have said these things to you," he told his disciples, "so that my joy may be in you, and that your joy may be complete" (Jn 15:11). He prayed that their sorrow would be turned to joy (see Jn 17:13), and his prayer was answered on Easter Sunday. "The disciples rejoiced when they saw the Lord" (Jn 20:20).

"Sunday," John Paul II observes, "as a weekly echo of the first encounter with the Risen Lord, is unfailingly marked by the joy with which the disciples greeted the Master" (*Dies Domini*, 56). So as we approach each celebration of the Eucharist, this note of happiness and joy ought to affect our moods. In times of sorrow, pain, and fear, we should look to Jesus for comfort and courage. In times of despair, for hope. In times of peace and tranquillity, for an even greater measure of the joy that flows from the heart of Jesus.

THE COMMANDMENT

Anyone driving in the West knows to expect a lot of empty space between towns, and it is not unusual to see signs such as "Next services: 75 miles." Those who ignore such signs without checking the gas gauge do so at their own peril! As we travel the road of life, we ignore God's directions at our own peril. Among the most important of these directions are the Ten Commandments (see Ex 20:1–20; Deut 5:1–21). The third of these has a special relevance for us as we traverse life's pathways: "Observe the sabbath day, to keep it holy."

The Ten Commandments were designed by a loving God who knows what is best for us. God gave us freedom so we could love. Just as caring parents offer guidance to their children to keep them from harm, God offers guidance to keep us from falling into the slavery of sin. Some people wrongly assume that the commandments restrict our freedom. The truth is that they help us stay free. The third commandment is meant to keep us from becoming slaves to work and to the foolish notion that we can find lasting happiness without God. In the Book of Genesis, God establishes a pattern by creating the world in six days, then "resting" on the seventh. What is good for God is good for us.

For the Jews, the seventh day was the Sabbath (rest). Faithful Jews did no unnecessary work on the Sabbath, and they worshiped God with Scripture reading and prayer. Jesus kept the Sabbath by going to the synagogue to praise God and teach (see Mk 1:21; Lk 4:16). After his Resurrection, believers remembered that he had proclaimed himself "Lord of the sabbath" (Mt 12:8). They knew he had risen from the dead on the first day of the week, Sunday, appearing to his apostles that evening and on the following Sunday (see Jn 20:19, 26). He thereby established a new day of rest, the "Lord's day." The first Christians met "to break bread" (celebrate the Lord's Supper) on "the first day of the week," Sunday, as Scripture (see Acts 20:7; 1 Cor 16:1–2) and early Christian teachers testify. Saint Ignatius of Antioch, about A.D. 100, wrote to the Magnesians: "Those who lived by the ancient customs attained a fresh hope. They no longer observed Saturday, but Sunday, the Lord's day, for on that day life arose for us through Christ." (The letter may be found at ccel.org/fathers2/ANF-01-17.htm#P1394_249090; accessed January 12, 2011.)

We ought, then, to regard the words of the third commandment as a special gift of God. After all, they are God's own directions to keep us safe and secure on the road of life.

THE ONLY THING
JESUS ASKS US TO DO FOR HIM

Yet another reason we Catholics go to Mass is that it is the only thing Jesus asks us to do for him. Jesus asks us to do many things for others and for ourselves, but only one thing for him—the Eucharist. "This is my body, which is given for you. Do this in remembrance of me" (Lk 22:19). How can we be loyal followers of Jesus if we fail to do this one thing?

"I can be a good Catholic without going to Mass." This statement is simply untrue. We cannot be good Catholics unless we do what Jesus asks of us.

"I can pray at home, or in the woods. I don't need to go to Mass." These words are heard often. It is true that we can pray at home or in the woods. But it is not true that we don't need to go to Mass. We are not the ones to decide what sort of worship God desires. God is, and God tells us that private prayer is not enough. We need to pray in private (see Mt 6:6), but we must also pray with others (see Mt 18:20). Private prayer is essential to our spiritual growth, but essential also is prayer with others, especially the prayer mandated by Jesus at the Last Supper.

Some people say, "I'm spiritual, but not religious. I don't need Mass. I find God while hiking in the woods." But at the Last Supper, Jesus didn't say, "Go take a hike in memory of me." Sadly, those who don't come to Mass are saying to God, "Go take a hike. I don't have time for your requests." If we want to be true followers of Jesus, we will first celebrate the Eucharist in his memory, then go on our hike!

THE CHURCH AND MASS ATTENDANCE

The *Catechism of the Catholic Church* lists a number of precepts of the Church, laws meant to point out obligations we must fulfill so that we can grow in love of God and neighbor. The first of these precepts is "You shall attend Mass on Sundays and holy days of obligation, and rest from servile labor" (CCC 2041). In this precept the Church is only pointing out what God has commanded, what Christ asks of us, what Christians have done for twenty centuries. To ignore this and deliberately miss Mass unless excused by a serious reason (such as illness or care of sick children) is to disobey God. This, as the *Catechism* points out, is a grave sin (CCC 2180–2183).

The *Catechism* states that on Sundays and holy days of obligation Catholics should refrain from unnecessary work that would hinder the worship owed to God. We need leisure to rest from our labors and turn mind and heart to God (CCC 2184–2188).

The Church has the right and responsibility to clarify the obligations of its members. In speaking to the first leaders of the Church, Jesus said: "Whoever listens to you listens to me" (Lk 10:16) "and whatever you bind on earth will be bound in heaven" (Mt 16:19). We should hear the voice of Jesus himself in the first precept of the Church, for it is he who speaks through his Church.

But the Lord's day is much more than obligations! Sunday should be a time, as Pope John Paul II reminds us, to imitate the delight God took in the works of creation, especially humanity. As God contemplated humanity with love and joy on a "day of rest," so we should find joy in contemplating God and the beauty of nature. The Jewish people rejoiced also in God's saving works that freed them from slavery and led them into the Promised Land. We should find happiness in remembering Christ's death and Resurrection that freed us from the power of death and brought us hope of eternal joy (see *Dies Domini*, 8–30).

GOD ASKS SO LITTLE

God asks so little of us. If we live to be eighty, we'll spend about three years reading, five years talking, six years getting an education, six years riding in a car, seven years eating, eleven years in recreational activities, fourteen years working, and twenty-seven years sleeping. Attending Mass for an hour every week and praying five minutes every day adds up to...six months. How can we refuse so little to a loving God who has given us so much?

MASS IS GOOD FOR US

Attending Mass is good for us. In 1999, Duke University studies showed that regular church attendance can enhance physical, emotional, and mental health (ncbi.nlm.nih.gov/pubmed/10462170; accessed January 12, 2011). The effect of regular worship on survival has been equivalent to that of wearing versus not wearing seat belts in auto accidents, and of not smoking versus smoking (see Duke University Center for Spirituality, Theology and Health: spiritualityandhealth.duke.edu/; accessed January 12, 2011).

Dr. Daniel Hall, M.D., conducted a study at the University of Pittsburgh Medical Center indicating that regular church attendance can add two to three years of life. Dr. Hall noted that the effects of church attendance were similar to those of cholesterol-lowering medications, but without the cost (jabfm.org/cgi/content/abstract/19/2/103, accessed January 12, 2011). God knows what's best: Going to Mass every week takes six months of your life, and it may add two to three years!

CRUISE CONTROL

In many ways, Mass is like a car's cruise control. Cruise control can keep a car at seventy miles per hour whether it's going up a hill or down. Christ's peace keeps us steady in the ups and downs of life. Mass is a time to put our lives on cruise control. If we are angry or upset, Mass is a time to calm down in the gentle presence of Jesus. If we are weary, Mass is a time to be revived with the grace and life of Jesus. No matter what our mood, Christ's peace, granted at every Mass, can be a steadying influence which brings us the calm and courage we need to carry on.

IS MY WORLD BIG ENOUGH?

When considering the reasons for attending Mass, each of us should ask some important questions. Is my world big enough? Or do I limit it to what can be seen and touched? Do I act as if my life included only what I've experienced in the material world? Do I realize that I belong to a larger family, the Body of Christ, that I have homes (parish churches) all over the world, brothers and sisters who have needs and concerns like mine? Scripture says: "So...you are citizens with the saints and also members of the household of God, built upon the foundation of the apostles and prophets, with Christ Jesus himself as the cornerstone. In him the whole structure is joined together and grows into a holy temple in the Lord; in whom you also are built together spiritually into a dwelling place for God" (Eph 2:19–22). Mass both expresses and strengthens the reality of this larger family.

Do I recall that angels and saints in heaven love me and pray with me? Is Jesus part of my daily life, Jesus...the Savior who strengthens me, the Friend with whom I often converse, the Lord I serve in every thought, word, and deed? Mass places these beautiful truths before us, for it is at Mass that we come to "the city of the living God, the heavenly Jerusalem, and to innumerable angels in festal gathering, and to the assembly of the firstborn who are enrolled in heaven, and to God the judge of all, and to the spirits of the righteous made perfect, and to

Jesus, the mediator of a new covenant" (Heb 12:22–24). As we worship Christ on earth, we are one with angels and saints who worship him in heaven.

Mass is an opportunity to widen our horizons, to place things in perspective by weighing them on the scale of God's value system. Mass is a time to strengthen our bonds with the members of our Church family on earth and in heaven. Mass is a sacred moment to let the love and grace of Jesus flow into our very being, remembering that we are as dependent on him as branches are to the vine (see Jn 15:5), and that we can reach our true destiny only through him.

WORSHIPING THE TRUE GOD

Actions speak louder than words. In no area is this more true than in one's attitude toward worship. We "measure God" by our actions. If God isn't worth an hour on the weekend, if we refuse to give God the one gift Jesus asks ("Do this in memory of me"), our God is too small. Missing Mass is like looking through binoculars from the wrong end. God, and everything else that's truly important, will be minimized and reduced to insignificance.

We may say we believe in God. We may think we worship God. But if the God we claim to know and worship is not worth an hour of our time each week, then we cannot be in touch with the real God. Why? Because the real God is certainly worth that hour—and much more! If our "god" is so small that an hour at Mass seems inconvenient or unimportant, this "god" cannot be the true God but rather a little "godlet" we've put on a shelf to control and use as we please.

The true God made the universe, loves us with an everlasting love, and gave us these years on earth so that we might expand our horizons and become capable of seeing God face to face in heaven. Mass allows us to see God clearly, up close and personal.

EXAMINING OUR VALUE SYSTEM

When are we excused from attending Mass? As the *Catechism* points out, we are not obliged to attend Mass in certain situations, such as when we are ill or need to care for a sick child. Indeed, sometimes we should *not* go to Mass. Those who have the flu, for example, should stay at home, not just because they are sick, but because they might pass on their illness to others. The parent of a sick child should care for that child, and this responsibility takes precedence over the Mass obligation.

But real reasons should be distinguished from mere excuses. We can be tempted to skip Mass when we should attend. Perhaps we are just tired, or want to get an early start at the golf course. Or we may find ourselves in a situation where we find it difficult to make a decision about attending. Perhaps we are on vacation, and the nearest Catholic church is fifteen miles away. Should we go?

One way to decide is to ask: "If I were offered a week's wages to attend Mass this morning, would I go?" If my answer is yes, then I should attend Mass. Otherwise, I show that obedience to God's commandments is less important to me than money. Two considerations flow from such a decision. First, I've made money into an idol, a false god. Second, if my idea of God is someone worth less than a week's wages, I am out of touch with the true God, who is worth infinitely more than any amount of money!

GETTING THE MOST OUT OF LIFE

We began this chapter on a battlefield and quickly moved from there to the meaning of life and the vastness of God's universe. God was present to those young soldiers huddled near their makeshift altars, and God is present to the entire universe. God, whose power and love stretch beyond the limits of our imagination, came into our world in the person of Jesus Christ. Jesus gives us the Mass so that we may touch God and be touched by God. The Mass is not a mere obligation. It is a miracle that opens untold possibilities for us.

Gerald Schroeder, a scientist with a doctorate in physics from the Massachusetts Institute of Technology, now teaches Scripture in Jerusalem. In his fine book, *The Science of God,* he moves from a description of creation to the possibilities for joy the Creator holds out to us...

> *Let's look at the universe, its cosmic genesis, and see if we can discern hints of a transcendent Creator histori-cally active in the creation. If we do, we can move on and investigate how we might capture the all-too-rare rush of joy sensed when we chance upon the transcendent. Instead of waiting passively for it to happen, imagine being able to have that joy as a permanent partner in life. That would be called getting the most out of life* (p. 19).

Of all the places on earth where we might meet God, only at Mass is God most available to us. At Mass we recall the events at which God has been historically active in our world. At Mass Jesus, the Son of God, offers to the Father the most precious gift imaginable, himself. Made one with Jesus by God the Holy Spirit, we are privileged to join our lives to the offering of Jesus. With Jesus we are taken into the arms of the Father and enveloped in the love of the Holy Spirit. At Mass, instead of waiting passively for the "all-too-rare rush of joy sensed when we chance upon the transcendent," we accept the gift of union with God made possible by Jesus, and we accept in faith his joy "as a permanent partner in life." Mass is nothing less than "getting the most out of life!"

QUESTIONS FOR DISCUSSION AND REFLECTION

Which of the reasons for attending Mass are the most convincing to you? Which are the least convincing? What reasons for attending Mass would you add to those given in this chapter? Have you ever considered the fact that Mass is the only thing Jesus asked us to do for him? What do you think Gerald Schroeder means by "the all-too-rare rush of joy sensed when we chance upon the transcendent"? Have you ever experienced such a rush of joy? Is Mass an appropriate occasion for anticipating such an experience?

ACTIVITIES

Jesus' request at the Last Supper, "Do this in remembrance of me" (Lk 22:19), is closely linked to a question we find in the sixth chapter of John's Gospel. Jesus speaks to a large crowd about his gift of himself as the Living Bread and about his beautiful offer of intimate union with believers: "Those who eat my flesh and drink my blood abide in me, and I in them" (Jn 6:56). Many of his listeners reject his words and walk away. Jesus turns to his apostles and asks, "Do you also wish to go away?"

Spend a few minutes meditating on these two scenes, and talk to Jesus about how he must have felt when so many listeners walked away. Pray for those Catholics who have walked away from the Mass and no longer attend. Ask Jesus' pardon for any times you have taken his gift of the Eucharist for granted or participated at Mass without proper devotion.

Chapter Two

THE MASS: YESTERDAY, TODAY, AND FOREVER

~⚜~

W hen my Aunt Lena celebrated her one-hundredth birthday at a nursing home in Saint Louis, Missouri, I was
privileged to offer Mass for her in her room. Also present were
several of her children and grandchildren. As I held up the host
after the consecration, Aunt Lena whispered, as she always did
at Mass, "My Lord and my God."

Aunt Lena's love for the Mass had a long history, stretching
back to her childhood. There were special moments such as her
first holy Communion, but most times Mass was simply a part
of her life. She remained faithful to the Mass, passing on to her
children her love of Jesus and her dedication to his request that
we observe the Eucharist in memory of him.

The words she whispered at every consecration had a long
history too. They were first spoken by the apostle Thomas a week
after Jesus rose from the dead. Thomas had been absent when
Jesus appeared to the other apostles on Easter Sunday evening,
and he refused to accept their word that Christ had risen. "I'll
never believe," Thomas protested, "unless I can see his wounds,
place my fingers in the nail marks, and my hand into his side"
(see Jn 20:25). His doubts vanished when Jesus appeared, inviting
him to touch his risen body. Thomas fell to his knees and cried
out, "My Lord and my God" (see Jn 20:28).

The Mass has a long history as well, rooted in the passion, death, and Resurrection of Jesus, in his Easter appearances, and in events that happened long before Jesus was born. This living history can help us understand the Mass and appreciate how it brings the power of Christ's life, death, and Resurrection to the present day.

FROM SLAVERY TO FREEDOM: THE PASCHAL MEAL

The history of the Mass begins with the crack of a whip and the clanking of chains. The Hebrew people had been slaves in Egypt for so long that slavery seemed to be their natural condition. Then God inspired a Hebrew who had been raised in Pharaoh's palace to lead the slaves to a land of freedom that hundreds of years earlier God had given to Abraham, their father in faith. When Moses went to Pharaoh and demanded liberty for his people, Pharaoh ridiculed him and increased the harshness of their cruel slavery. Even a series of plagues could not force Pharaoh to change his mind.

Then, the Bible relates, God told Moses there would be a final plague, the death of the firstborn of all the Egyptians. The Hebrews were to prepare for flight. To protect themselves from the destroying angel who would afflict the Egyptians, the Hebrews were to slaughter a lamb and smear its blood on the doorposts of their houses. This would cause the angel to "pass over" their homes when he struck down the firstborn of their oppressors. They were to eat the lamb with unleavened bread and bitter herbs. They were to repeat this meal each year to commemorate their deliverance from slavery (see Ex 12:1–28; Deut 16:1–8).

The Hebrews fled from Egypt and spent forty years wandering in the desert before finally arriving in the land promised them by God. After this exodus, they continued to observe the directives given by Moses for the Passover meal. Each year, they read the Scriptures relating the story of their deliverance. They sacrificed a lamb and recalled how the blood of a lamb had saved their ancestors from death. They ate the traditional meal and prayed the traditional words, thus feeding body and soul, and strengthening their bond with God and one another. As they went through centuries of struggle and oppression, the Passover began to anticipate the full redemption God would one day bring them through a savior, an anointed one, the Messiah.

JESUS AND THE PASSOVER

More than a thousand years after Moses led the Hebrews out of slavery, the long-awaited Messiah came. Jesus preached a gospel of love and mercy, telling of God's desire to make all nations a chosen people. This message infuriated some powerful Jewish leaders, who could not tolerate the notion that God loved even their enemies. They feared that their status and security were threatened by Jesus' teaching of a new covenant that would replace the temple worship over which they presided. Over time, their hatred of Jesus grew until they would be satisfied only by his death. Jesus knew this, but he continued to preach. He refused to use his divine power to crush them, relying only on love to call them to repentance. They failed to respond, and Jesus began to warn his followers that he would be put to death.

Eventually, Jesus decided to go to Jerusalem to face his enemies. He went at Passover time on the first day of the week and was welcomed by huge throngs who acclaimed him as Messiah. This only intensified the resolve of his foes to eliminate him. They could not risk arresting him publicly because of his popularity, but Judas Iscariot, one of Jesus' apostles, offered to betray him for thirty pieces of silver. They agreed and waited for an opportunity to apprehend Jesus.

It came on Thursday. Jesus, knowing that those who hated him were closing in, did not run. Instead, he sent Peter and John to prepare the Passover meal at the home of a friend. That evening he gathered with his twelve apostles for the Passover. He washed their feet as an expression of his love for them. He led them in the prayers and Scripture readings. He stunned them with the revelation that one of them would betray him. He did this, perhaps in an effort to dissuade Judas from his treachery, but Judas slipped away to carry out his plot.

So this Passover related not only to the celebration of the Exodus from Egypt, the journey from slavery to freedom. It was also bound to the new Exodus of Jesus, his journey from this world to the next, from death to life. It was linked to Jesus' sacrifice of his life to bring all people from the slavery of sin into the freedom of God's love. In this framework of Exodus, old and new, Jesus instituted the Eucharist, showing the connection between this "Last Supper" and what would happen the following day.

"Then he took a loaf of bread, and when he had given thanks, he broke it and gave it to them, saying, 'This is my body, which is given for you. Do this in remembrance of me'" (Lk 22:19). "Then he took a cup, and after giving thanks he gave it to them, saying, 'Drink from it, all of you; for this is my blood of the covenant, which is poured out for many for the forgiveness of sins'" (Mt 26:27–28).

THE LAMB OF GOD

When Jesus took the bread and transformed it into his body, he identified it with his body that would be sacrificed the next day: "This is my body, which is given for you." When he took the cup of wine and said, "This is my blood of the covenant, which is poured out for many for the forgiveness of sins," he identified it with his blood to be shed on the cross.

The bond between the Last Supper and Calvary can be seen also in the fact that Jesus became a new paschal lamb, sacrificed to save us from death. The prophet Isaiah foretold the coming of an obedient servant who would give his life as an offering for sin. The servant would be like "a lamb that is led to the slaughter" (Isa 53:7). John the Baptist surely had this in mind when he pointed out Jesus as the "Lamb of God who takes away the sin of the world!" (Jn 1:29). The deacon Philip used Isaiah's prophecy of the lamb led to slaughter to explain the good news of Jesus' death and Resurrection (see Acts 8:29–39). The First Letter of Peter states that we have been ransomed "with the precious blood of Christ, like that of a lamb without defect or blemish" (1:19). The Book of Revelation refers to Jesus as a Lamb more than thirty times, a Lamb that had been slain (see 5:6) and a Lamb once on a cross but now enthroned in heaven as Lord and God (see 22:1, 3).

THE BREAKING OF THE BREAD

This explains why the first Christians did not observe all the ceremonies for the Jewish paschal meal when keeping Jesus' commandment to "do this in remembrance of me." There was no need to shed the blood of another sacrificial lamb. They knew that the true Paschal Lamb had been slain and that his death sufficed for the salvation of the world. "For our paschal lamb, Christ, has been sacrificed" (1 Cor 5:7).

Instead, the early Christians took bread and wine and repeated the words of Jesus. This action made present for them the power of Christ's death and Resurrection. Paul observes: "For as often as you eat this bread and drink the cup, you proclaim the Lord's death until he comes" (1 Cor 11:26).

The name they gave to their memorial of the Last Supper was, as we saw in the Introduction (p. 4), the *breaking of the bread*.

They derived their pattern for this rite not only from Jesus' words and actions on Holy Thursday, but also from what may be called the first Mass celebrated after the Resurrection (CCC 1347).

It was Easter Sunday evening. Two of Jesus' disciples were walking to a village called Emmaus, about seven miles from Jerusalem. They were talking about the events of the previous week when the risen Jesus appeared to them. But he appeared in such a way that they did not recognize him. Jesus asked them what they were discussing. One of them, Cleopas, remarked that this stranger must be the only one in the area who didn't know what had been happening. He then told Jesus about the crucifixion and about rumors they'd heard of an empty tomb—rumors in which they'd apparently placed little confidence.

Jesus proceeded to describe the prophecies of Scripture that had foretold his sufferings, death, and Resurrection. He obviously got their attention, because when he acted as if he were continuing past their destination, they begged him to stay with them. He did, and he rewarded them for their hospitality. "When he was at table with them, he took bread, blessed and broke it, and gave it to them. Then their eyes were opened, and they recognized him; and he vanished from their sight" (Lk 24:30–31). In their excitement, as they recalled how their hearts had been burning as Jesus talked to them on the road, they rushed back to Jerusalem with the news that they had seen Jesus. There "they told what had happened on the road, and how he had been made known to them in the breaking of the bread" (Lk 24:35).

THE PASCHAL MYSTERY

What Jesus revealed to the two disciples was the Paschal Mystery. His death on the cross was not an execution forced upon him by enemies. Rather, it was his gift to the Father. He chose to accept death rather than to stop proclaiming God's mercy. This choice represents the greatest act of love in the history of humanity. It broke down the barriers that sin had built between us and God. And because Jesus was God, death could not hold him. He rose from the grave, to be exalted at God's right hand forever. The Paschal Mystery, then, is Christ's passion and death, Resurrection, and Ascension. It is a mystery because the love it reveals is beyond human comprehension.

In Christ's "opening the Scriptures" to the two disciples on the road to Emmaus, in his prayer of thanks at the meal, and in the breaking of the bread, the early Church discerned a pattern for celebrating the Paschal Mystery, the Eucharist. The celebration included a Liturgy of the Word and a Liturgy of the Eucharist. The first Christians found Christ, just as we do today, in Scripture and in receiving the bread that is Jesus. At every Eucharist, they remembered and celebrated, as we do, the Paschal Mystery.

THE MASS AFTER
CHRIST'S ASCENSION

After Christ ascended into heaven, his closest followers gathered in Jerusalem and devoted themselves to prayer, awaiting the coming of the Holy Spirit promised by the Lord. When the Spirit descended on them at Pentecost, they began to preach the Good News with enthusiasm. Mass was a part of their lives as described by Luke: "They devoted themselves to the apostles' teaching and fellowship, to the breaking of bread and the prayers" (Acts 2:42). At first, they also participated in temple worship. "Day by day, as they spent much time together in the temple, they broke bread at home" (Acts 2:46). Here, as for the disciples at Emmaus, there was a Liturgy of the Word (the Scriptures and prayer at the temple or synagogue) and the Liturgy of the Eucharist (the breaking of the bread).

But when Jewish leaders initiated a persecution of Christians, the followers of Jesus gradually separated themselves from Jewish temple and synagogue worship. Paul, a persecutor converted to Christianity by a vision of Jesus, preached the gospel among Gentiles and celebrated the Eucharist with them. We read of one such celebration in Troas, a city in Asia Minor. There the Christians met in an upper room "to break bread." Paul preached so long that a young man, Eutychus, began to doze off and fell three floors to the ground below. Fortunately, Paul, who had caused the boy's death with his lengthy sermon, was able to bring him back to life by the power of God (see Acts 20:6–12).

In his writings, Paul informs us of early Christian attitudes toward the Eucharist and explains how communities celebrated the Mass. He demonstrates their belief in the reality of Christ's eucharistic presence and in its power to join believers to Jesus and one another: "The cup of blessing that we bless, is it not a sharing in the blood of Christ? The bread that we break, is it not a sharing in the body of Christ? Because there is one bread, we who are many are one body, for we all partake of the one bread" (1 Cor 10:16–17). Paul also shows how the Eucharist was joined to a community meal intended to give wealthy Christians an opportunity to share with the poor.

The meal, however, gave rise to abuses. Paul had to chastise the Corinthians because they ate their own food instead of sharing. Some imbibed so much they become drunk. Their meals produced divisions rather than unity. "What!" he implores, "Do you not have homes to eat and drink in? Or do you show contempt for the church of God and humiliate those who have nothing?"

(1 Cor 11:17–22). They ought to know better, Paul implies, for the Eucharist is a gift from Jesus himself.

As evidence, Paul gives the first description of the Last Supper, found in 1 Corinthians 11:23–26, a passage written about twenty-five years after Christ's Resurrection.

For I received from the Lord what I also handed on to you, that the Lord Jesus on the night when he was betrayed took a loaf of bread, and when he had given thanks, he broke it and said, "This is my body that is for you. Do this in remembrance of me." In the same way he took the cup also, after supper, saying, "This cup is the new covenant in my blood. Do this, as often as you drink it, in remembrance of me" (1 Cor 11:23–25).

Paul shows that the first Christians realized the link between the Mass and Christ's death and Resurrection. "For as often as you eat this bread and drink the cup, you proclaim the Lord's death until he comes" (1 Cor 11:26). He teaches that such a gift as the Eucharist must be reverenced, for whoever "eats the bread or drinks the cup of the Lord in an unworthy manner will be answerable for the body and blood of the Lord" (1 Cor 11:27).

Just how long the Christians celebrated the Eucharist in the context of a meal is uncertain. But there is an interesting hint in the New Testament that it was not for an extended period. When Paul describes the Last Supper, he states that the consecration of the wine took place "after supper." Luke, a disciple of Paul, does the same in his Gospel. But Mark and Matthew, perhaps reflecting a later practice when no meal was celebrated with the Eucharist, show the consecration of bread and wine one after the other, not divided by the supper.

HANDING DOWN THE EUCHARIST

When the apostles celebrated their first Masses, they presumably spoke the same language Jesus did at the Last Supper, Aramaic. But soon Christians were celebrating Mass in Greek as well. There were probably more Jews living outside Palestine than in the Holy Land. Most of them spoke Greek and used a Greek translation of the Jewish Scriptures. When Paul and other disciples began to preach to such Jews and to non-Jewish peoples, they spoke Greek. They wrote the entire New Testament, including Jesus' words at the Last Supper, in Greek.

It is likely, then, that the language at most Masses during the time of the apostles was Greek. Mass prayers were probably modeled on Jewish Passover prayers of remembrance, praise, and thanks, and on those commonly used in the synagogues, such as the "holy, holy, holy" of Isaiah 6:3. Some Hebrew words of these prayers, such as *Amen* and *Alleluia,* were retained and are still used today.

In A.D. 70 the Romans destroyed the city of Jerusalem, leveling its temple. (Note: All dates in this book will henceforth be given without the A.D.) Christians now saw themselves more clearly as people of the "New Covenant" (see Heb 10:8–10). The Old Testament prophecy of a pure offering to God from all the nations (see Mal 1:11) was being realized as they celebrated the Eucharist. But they did not reject their roots. The New Covenant was built on the Old, and Christians continued to use the Jewish Scriptures at Mass along with the writings of the apostles (see Col 4:16). An early Christian document, the *Didache* (which means "Instruction") contains prayers used at the meal before the Eucharist and perhaps at the Eucharist itself. These prayers reflect their Jewish background.

The *Didache* does not give examples of what today are called eucharistic prayers. Apparently, those presiding offered prayers of their own composition, except for the words of consecration.

There seem to have been at least two patterns for these words, as was noted previously. The first is that found in Matthew 26:26–29 and Mark 14:22–26, the second in Luke 22:19–20 and 1 Corinthians 11:23–26. These two patterns may have been preserved in celebrations of the Mass before they were written down in Scripture. (You will find more information on the *Didache* in the *Catholic Encyclopedia* at newadvent.org/cathen/; accessed January 12, 2011.)

A NEW GENERATION

Before the death of the last apostle, Christians established communities of believers in Palestine, Asia Minor, northern Africa, Greece, Spain, and Italy. They met at private homes as "churches" identified by the owner (see Rom 16:5; Col 4:15; Philem vs. 2), where bishops, assisted by priests and deacons, led the people in worship. A community of Christians existed in Rome, the dominant power in the Mediterranean area (see Rom 16). Unfortunately, they drew the attention of the emperor Nero, a madman who launched a bloody persecution in 64, killing Peter, Paul, and many other Christians. The persecution ended with Nero's suicide in 68, but another sprang up under the emperor Domitian (81–96). This persecution was widespread, and it established an official policy under which Christians were liable to arrest, confiscation of property, slavery, torture, and death.

The deaths of Peter, the first bishop of Rome, and of Paul, the great teacher of the Gentiles, gave notice that the apostolic era was drawing to a close. John, who outlived the other apostles, died around the turn of the century. By then, nearly half a million people from India to western Europe called themselves Christian. As those who had seen Christ in person passed away, the next generation must have wondered what the future would hold.

They must also have looked back to Jesus' first followers, many of whom had died a martyr's death, as heroes. But the Christians of New Testament times were not perfect. They struggled to believe that Jesus loved them enough to make himself truly present in the Eucharist (see Jn 6). They allowed abuses to creep into their worship, and had to be corrected by their leaders (see 1 Cor). Some of them stopped coming to the eucharistic assembly (see Heb 10:25). They struggled to live the faith in an empire hostile to their values and beliefs. But in spite of persecution and their own weaknesses, they handed on the Eucharist they had received from Jesus.

They handed on as well, in the Book of Revelation and elsewhere, their conviction that the Eucharist had cosmic dimensions. When Christians on earth worshiped the Lamb of God, they were joined by heavenly dwellers, who offered the prayers of those on earth to God like incense (see Rev 5:8). The hymns Christians sang in praise of God on earth were echoed by the voices of angels in heaven. "Every creature in heaven and on earth...[sang] 'To the one seated on the throne and to the Lamb / be blessing and honor and glory and might / forever and ever!'" (Rev 5:13).

THE POST-APOSTOLIC CHURCH

The Corinthians, who had caused Saint Paul so much distress by bad conduct at meals before the Eucharist, were misbehaving again as the first century drew to a close. In Paul's time, they had allowed personal rivalries to divide their community (see 1 Cor 1:10–14). Now they were rebelling against the bishop and priests set over their Church.

In 96, Saint Clement, the bishop of Rome, wrote to the Corinthians, chiding them for their insurgence. "Indeed, it will be no small sin for us," he affirmed, "if we oust men who have irreproachably and piously offered the sacrifices proper to the episcopate." After referring to the various levels of priesthood in Jewish temple worship (high priest, Levites, and laity), he stated that Christians, too, must attend to the various levels of ministry (bishop, priest, and deacon) as they celebrated the Eucharist. Clement's letter before the close of the first century shows that the Church believed the Eucharist should be offered by the proper ministers; that it was regarded as a sacrifice; and that the ministry of bishops, priests, and deacons came not from the community but from God. The letter also indicates that early Christians regarded the bishop of Rome as possessing special authority over the life and worship of Churches outside Rome. No hint can be found that the Corinthians felt Clement was exceeding his rights when he corrected them. (Clement's *First Epistle to the Corinthians* may be found at ccel.org/ccel/schaff/anf01.toc.html; accessed January 12, 2011.)

Ten years later, Saint Ignatius of Antioch wrote to the church at Philadelphia a letter expressing Christian belief about the Mass. He told them to observe one Eucharist because the Body of Christ is one and because there is one altar of sacrifice and one bishop, assisted by clergy and deacons. In a letter to the Smyrnaeans, he warned against heretics who had left the Church because they would not profess "the Eucharist to be the flesh of our Savior Jesus Christ, which suffered for our sins, and which the Father, of his goodness, raised up again." (Both letters may be found at ccel.org/ccel/schaff/anf01.toc.html [scroll down to "Ignatius"; accessed January 12, 2011.)

For more than one hundred years after the Resurrection, Christians did not describe the details of their eucharistic gatherings to outsiders. The Mass was regarded as such a special gift that it could be revealed only to the baptized. But in the middle of the second century, Saint Justin the Martyr broke the silence. He had been a pagan philosopher and was highly regarded for his wisdom. He wrote an explanation of Christian beliefs to the emperor, Antoninus Pius, and to the emperor's son, Marcus Aurelius, in an effort to convince them that Christians were not the evildoers portrayed by enemies. In his *Apologia* (which means "explanation") he described the Eucharist in these words:

On the day we call the day of the sun, all who dwell in the city or country gather in the same place. The memoirs of the apostles and the writings of the prophets are read, as much as time permits. When the reader has finished, he who presides over those gathered admonishes and challenges them to imitate these beautiful things. Then we all rise together and offer prayers for ourselves...and for all others, wherever they may be, so that we may be found righteous by our life and actions, and faithful to the commandments, so as to obtain eternal salvation. When the prayers are concluded we exchange the kiss. Then someone brings bread and a cup of water and wine mixed together to him who presides over the brethren. He takes them and offers praise and glory to the Father of the universe, through the name of the Son and of the Holy Spirit and for a considerable time he gives thanks (in Greek: eucharistian) that we have been judged worthy of these gifts. When he has concluded the prayers and thanksgivings, all present give voice to an acclamation by saying: "Amen." When he who presides has given thanks and the people have responded, those whom we call deacons give to those present the "eucharisted" bread, wine and water and take them to those who are absent. (Saint Justin, Apologia, cited in CCC 1345. The document may be found at catholic-forum.com/saints/ stj29002.htm; accessed January 12, 2011.)

The similarities between the Mass in Justin's time and the Mass of today are obvious. In fact, if we were suddenly transported to a eucharistic assembly in the middle of the second century, we would no doubt feel very much at home. We would join others gathering together in one place on Sunday. A priest (called the *president*, or the one who presides), assisted by deacons, would lead the congregation in prayer. We would hear the reading of passages from the Old and New Testaments and the General Intercessions. Next would come a collection, the bringing up of gifts (some of which would later be distributed to the poor), the eucharistic prayer said by the priest and affirmed by the people with an *Amen*, and holy Communion. As Mass ended, Communion would be taken to the sick who could not attend.

We would note differences as well. For example, the sign of peace would be earlier in the Mass than today. There would be no definite formula for prayers said over the gifts or for the eucharistic prayer. The words of Jesus at the Last Supper were certainly recited, but otherwise, as Justin's *Apologia* mentions, the priest offered "prayers and thanksgivings" (the eucharistic prayer) "according to his ability."

Justin had hoped to soften the stance of the Roman emperors toward Christians. Sadly, his effort failed in this regard, and he himself was executed by Marcus Aurelius. But his *Apologia* has been a great blessing to succeeding generations, as it demonstrates how the Mass of Christians who had known the apostles is one with the Mass of every age.

HIPPOLYTUS

Hippolytus was one of the most fascinating, colorful, and controversial characters of the early Church. The end of the second century found him as a priest-scholar at Rome. He spoke and wrote in Greek, the language of the educated upper class. In 217, a former slave by the name of Callistus was elected to the papacy. He was a holy man, highly respected by the people. Because of his background, he was sympathetic to the poor and lowly, and he decided that the Eucharist could be offered in Latin, the language of the common people. Up to this time, Greek had been the language of the Mass, except in churches in North Africa. Hippolytus favored Greek, and he was so upset at the change that he broke away and became the first antipope.

Callistus was martyred in 222. About ten years later, a new pope, Pontianus (also called Pontian), was exiled with Hippolytus to Sardinia. There Hippolytus and his followers were reconciled to the Church. Hippolytus died a martyr and is now honored as a saint.

Hippolytus is important to our study of the liturgy because he wrote a eucharistic prayer which was copied and used by other priests. This prayer served as a pattern for Eucharistic Prayer II in today's liturgy. Compare, for example, the words of Hippolytus (bombaxo.com/hippolytus.html, paragraph 31; accessed January 12, 2011) with these words from the preface of the Second Eucharistic Prayer:

The Lord be with you.
And with your spirit.

Lift up your hearts.
We lift them up to the Lord.

Let us give thanks to the Lord.
It is right and just.

It is truly right and just, our duty and our salvation,
always and everywhere to give you thanks, Father most holy,
through your beloved Son, Jesus Christ,
your Word through whom you made all things,
whom you sent as our Savior and Redeemer,
incarnate by the Holy Spirit and born of the Virgin.

Other eucharistic prayers were composed and circulated during and after the time of Hippolytus. However, the custom of allowing each priest to recite his own prayers remained common, as did the use of the Greek language. Greek was not generally replaced by Latin in the Roman liturgy until about a century after Hippolytus.

WORSHIP AND PERSECUTION

Because Christianity was a persecuted religion, Christians could not worship in public buildings. Instead, they usually met in the homes of believers, as in New Testament times. When the Eucharist was celebrated by small numbers in the context of a meal, those attending apparently sat at a table around the priest. After the meals were discontinued, and when the Christian communities grew larger, people would stand around the table as the priest celebrated the Eucharist. When persecutions were severe, Christians at times had to celebrate the Eucharist in secret locations, including the catacombs, underground burial places hollowed out of rock. Because tombs were carved into the walls of these caverns, the priest, celebrating Mass on the tomb of a martyr, would lead the prayers with his back to the people. Masses in or near catacombs were no doubt rare, and few could attend because of limited space.

But even in such places, Christians celebrated Mass only at great risk. During the persecution of Emperor Valerian, Roman soldiers trapped a group of Christians celebrating the Eucharist in a catacomb. They blockaded the entrances, then buried the Christians alive. After Pope Saint Stephen was cut down while celebrating Mass, his successor was martyred in a catacomb. Describing the death of Pope Sixtus II at the hands of Roman soldiers in 258, Saint Cyprian, bishop of Carthage, wrote: "I must...inform you that Sixtus was put to death in a catacomb on the sixth of August, and four deacons with him" (Epist. 80:CSEL, 3, 839–840, cited from *The Liturgy of the Hours,* IV, 1297). Cyprian was himself martyred a few weeks later.

Perhaps the harshest of the persecutions was instigated by Emperor Diocletian (284–305). By the end of his reign, tens of thousands of Christians had been martyred during a period lasting more than two centuries. Nevertheless, Christianity continued to spread, with several million believers at the start of the fourth century. And a dramatic change was about to take place, a change that would have an lasting impact on Catholic worship.

THE EDICT OF MILAN

Diocletian's death was followed by years of chaos, as several men struggled to gain the throne of the Roman Empire. Constantine, an army general, emerged as emperor. He credited his military victories to Christ's intervention and in 313 issued the Edict of Milan, which granted religious tolerance to Christians. He promoted Christianity throughout the empire and established a new capital city at Constantinople. Constantine donated many public buildings in Rome and elsewhere to the Church for worship, including his Lateran palace in Rome. This site is now the location of Saint John Lateran Basilica.

The large crowds that could now attend Mass at such churches necessitated a more organized liturgical structure. The Church began to develop orders of worship and ceremonies for the celebration of sacraments. Spiritual leaders, such as John Chrysostom, Ambrose, Augustine, and Pope Gregory the Great, guided the Church in developing worship rites whose influences can be seen even today. Bishops began to compose booklets for their own use at Mass, and the best of these were circulated for use by others. One such work, attributed to Saint Ambrose in the late fourth century, includes a prayer similar to Eucharistic Prayer

I. Liturgical music, mostly in the form of plain chant, grew in importance.

Rome began to collapse in the fifth century as barbarian tribes from central and eastern Europe crossed her boundaries and invaded the once powerful Empire. At the close of this century the Frankish king Clovis converted to Christianity along with thousands of his people. Churches in France requested directions for celebrating the rites observed in Rome, and interaction between the Roman Church and France as well as other developing nations would influence liturgical practice for centuries.

Meantime, the eastern empire with its capital at Constantinople was growing weaker. In the seventh century the Church in the East came under the attack of Islamic armies; those armies then made inroads into Africa and Spain until turned back in 732 at Poitiers. The chaos of the times allowed for much liturgical diversification, and many different rites and languages developed in the East and the West. The eastern rites developed into permanent liturgies still celebrated today. In the West, the invading barbarian tribes, which had no written language and little culture, were inclined to adopt the Latin language of Roman bishops and administrators. Latin naturally became the language of the liturgy as the tribes settled down and formed cultures built around the traditions and sacramental structure already available in the Church.

This structure had been greatly improved by Gregory the Great, who served as pope from 590 to 604. Gregory was a brilliant scholar and an excellent administrator, and he condensed several liturgical books prepared by his predecessor, Pope Gelasius, into one coherent whole. By Gregory's time, the custom of the priest's improvising eucharistic prayers at each Mass had been replaced in Rome by a fixed formula, or canon. This canon of the Mass developed over time into what we now know as the First Eucharistic Prayer. Gregory organized ritual guidelines around this core and established a pattern of song and participation that would seem familiar to any Catholic of the twenty-first century.

At first, the elaborate ceremonies developed by Gregory remained localized in Rome. But the canon, ceremonies, Latin language, and chant of the Roman Mass had been well organized into a compelling structure, readily available in books that could be copied and distributed. As priests, monks, and others witnessed the beauty and order of the Roman liturgy, they wanted to bring this liturgy to their own cities and nations. In time, the Roman liturgy would become the norm for the Church in the western world.

Rites and the Roman Rite

The most important rites that existed along with the Roman were those of Milan (where Constantine promulgated his edict granting Christians freedom of worship), Spain, Ireland, and France. These rites had been influenced by eastern liturgies and allowed for more variety than the Roman rite. Their gradual transformation under the influence of the Roman rite can be traced in books called *sacramentaries,* which were hand copied in Rome and brought to various locations in Europe. These books contained the canon, some readings, and Mass prayers originating from popes of the sixth to the eighth centuries. They reveal how the Mass developed over the centuries.

Many of the warring tribes of Europe were united under Charlemagne (b 741?–d 814). A great warrior king, he ruled over a vast territory encompassing much of modern France, Germany, Spain, and northern Italy. A devout Catholic, he saw in the Roman liturgy a source of unity for the diverse tribes he now ruled. With the assistance of a monk, Alcuin, he oversaw the spread of the Roman rite throughout his empire.

Alcuin was wise enough to make adaptations based on the rites which already existed in the various regions. As a result the

Roman rite underwent changes which eventually found their way back to Rome itself. These revisions included greater participation by the congregation in the prayers and chant, recitation of the Creed on Sundays and holy days, the use of unleavened bread for the Eucharist, the practice of kneeling to receive Communion on the tongue, the ringing of bells, a gradual separation of the altar from the people, and an increase in gestures, such as genuflections, the Sign of the Cross, and incensing. The use of the pipe organ began at this time, and Charlemagne had one built in his private chapel.

The separation of the altar from the people may have been due to several factors. Kings, such as Charlemagne, were set apart from the people on lofty thrones. Christ was seen as the greatest king of all, and the altar was his throne. So that the altar might be surrounded with decorations, it was placed against a highly ornamented wall. The priest then prayed with his back to the people, as those celebrating Mass in the catacombs had done.

Many other issues are involved in the placement of the altar and direction of liturgical prayer. In some ancient churches, the priest and people prayed facing the East—where the sun rose, a symbol of Christ, Light of the world. Priest and people prayed, therefore, with their faces turned to Christ. (For an excellent discussion of these matters, see pages 74-84 of *The Spirit of the Liturgy*, by Joseph Cardinal Ratzinger (now Pope Benedict XVI), Ignatius Press.)

The interaction between the liturgy of Rome and the liturgies of developing nations in Europe continued for two hundred years after Charlemagne's death. But as different areas of Europe developed their own languages, Latin fell into disuse in everyday life except among the clergy and educated laity. Soon only the priest could read the Scriptures and prayers in Latin, and ordinary people came to Mass more as spectators than as participants. The Roman sacramentaries were condensed into one Latin missal, first in Germany and eventually in Rome.

MASS IN A NEW MILLENNIUM

The first millennium of Christianity saw the Mass expand from the Upper Room of the Last Supper to all parts of the civilized world. As the second millennium began, the Church in the West depended for its liturgy on a missal which contained prayers and ceremonies that had evolved over hundreds of years. The next four centuries would see little creative development in the liturgy of the Mass. But these countries would witness the construction of majestic Gothic cathedrals throughout Europe by which generations of believers would express their desire to place the Mass in the most magnificent setting possible. Saint Thomas Aquinas and other great theologians would help the Church to grow in its understanding of the Eucharist.

However, historical circumstances, a lack of education among the common people, confusion caused by heresies, and other factors tended to keep the participation of the people to a minimum. Chant at the Mass was limited to the priest and choir, while the people listened. Furthermore, reception of Communion, which had been on the decline for several centuries, became even less frequent, with some people receiving Communion only on their deathbed. But while people were reluctant to receive the host, they wanted to see Christ in the sacramental species, so the elevation of the host and chalice after the consecration became common practice.

The fourteenth century ushered in problems devastating to the life of the Church. Pope Clement V, a Frenchman, moved to Avignon in 1309, and his successors remained there until 1378. In 1378, the cardinals divided into factions, and a situation known as the Western Schism resulted. Two or three rivals claimed the papacy, and the matter was not settled until the election of Martin V in 1417. The Black Death (1346–1350) wiped out half the population in parts of Europe. War raged between France and England, and among many other countries as well.

The fifteenth century brought the flowering of the Renaissance, an era which saw the arts and sciences flourish and a secularism pervade all of society. With the Renaissance came the most worldly popes in the history of the Church: Pius II, Sixtus IV, Innocent VIII, Alexander VI, and Julius II. These men patronized major achievements in art and architecture, such as Saint Peter's Basilica and the Sistine Chapel, but their worldliness scandalized the faithful. Some bishops and priests followed the lead of these popes, and a general laxity and carelessness plagued the liturgy as a result. Many saintly Catholics, both clergy and laity, pleaded for renewal in liturgy and life, but their pleas went unheeded.

PROTESTANTISM AND THE COUNCIL OF TRENT

In 1517, Martin Luther, a Catholic monk, posted his Ninety-Five Theses on a chapel door in Wittenberg, Germany. At first he wanted reform, not a new Church. But poor communications, stubbornness on the part of Luther and his Catholic adversaries, and interference by secular authorities led him to adopt positions irreconcilable with Catholic theology. Luther denied, for example, the sacrificial nature of the Mass and the need for an ordained priesthood. He was followed in his break from the Church by Jean Calvin (Switzerland: Presbyterianism), John Knox (Scotland: Reformed churches), Henry VIII (England: Anglicanism, Episcopalianism), and others. While Luther maintained that Christ was present in the Eucharist, most of the others who left the Church denied the Real Presence. Each new Church remade its liturgy according to the theological whims of its founder and the language and culture of its own nation.

The Protestant revolt finally shocked Catholic leadership into serious efforts toward reform. The Council of Trent (1545–1563) clarified Catholic belief, corrected abuses, and set up the seminary system for the education of clergy. The saintly Pius V (1566–1572) promoted spiritual revival among the faithful and promulgated a new *Roman Missal.* The basis for this *Missal* was the one used in Rome. The texts, ceremonies, and chants of this *Missal* had the advantage of being well organized and time tested, but they also contained some anachronisms. For example, the celebrant would dismiss the people with the words, *Ite missa est,* then give the blessing, perhaps harking back to the time when the pope would dismiss the congregation, then bless people as he processed out of the church.

On July 14, 1570, Pope Pius V made the new *Missal* obligatory for the whole western Church, except in dioceses that had followed their own liturgy for two centuries or more. Pius V ruled that only authorized versions of the *Missal* could be used. Latin was the only language allowed. Changes to the approved text were forbidden.

The new *Missal* succeeded in providing a pattern for worship throughout the Catholic Church in the West and put an end to the abuses that had been rampant before the Council of Trent. It established a pattern for the Mass which remained almost unchanged until the middle of the twentieth century.

But the *Roman Missal* was far from perfect. Because Pius V wanted to initiate liturgical reform as quickly as possible, he did not mandate a study of liturgical practices in the early Church. Instead, he accepted rites and ceremonies which had developed over centuries by trial and error. Not all of these were liturgically ideal. The reception of Communion, for example, was adapted from the rite for Communion for the sick, including the *Confiteor* (I Confess) and two absolutions. Readings from Scripture were limited, with the same passages, in some instances, repeated every day of the week. Participation was limited to a dialogue between the priest and servers, or priest and choir, with the congregation observing the Mass in silence.

TRENT TO VATICAN II

The *Roman Missal* of Pius V was almost universally accepted throughout the western Church. Catholics were appalled at the divisions among Protestant churches, and they saw the value of forming a unified body behind the pope. Having one approved *Missal* that contained all the texts necessary for the Eucharist greatly simplified the responsibilities of bishops and priests when they prepared and celebrated the liturgy. It also meant that only one book had to be purchased by each parish church, an economical benefit when the printing of books was still in its infancy.

Sixtus V, who served as pope from 1585 to 1590, created a new department of the Roman Curia, the Congregation of Rites and Ceremonies, to see that the liturgy was properly celebrated throughout the western world. Detailed guidelines were laid down by experts on rubrics (rules for the liturgy, printed in red in the *Missals*, hence the word *rubric*, from the Latin word for "red"). Regulations were printed for every action in the Mass, from the proper way of bowing to the correct way of handing the priest an incense spoon.

The fear that aberrations might creep into the liturgy was so strong that translation of the Latin *Missal* into other languages was forbidden until the twentieth century. As a result, people used prayer books of various kinds or recited the rosary during Mass. Preaching declined in importance, partly because of the limited selection of readings in the *Missal*. When sermons were given, they might have no relationship to the Scripture readings of the day. Jansenism, a heretical movement originating with Flemish theologian Cornelis Jansen about 1640, taught an extreme rigorism and emphasized the fear of God to such an extent that many Catholics seldom received Communion. The introduction of musical instruments and the development of choral music at worship encouraged the creation of magnificent works such as Mozart's *Requiem*, but such works might be performed in a way that overshadowed the Mass itself. While the choir sang the Creed, for example, the priest might continue with the offertory prayers. All these circumstances tended to make the laity view the Mass as something to be attended, rather than a sacramental action in which they had a significant role to play.

Minor changes were made to the *Roman Missal* over the centuries. In 1604, Pope Clement VIII corrected printing errors, revised the translation of some prayers, and clarified rubrics. On several other occasions, popes revised prayers, added new Masses, and made other alterations, such as the prayers after Mass legislated by Leo XIII in 1884. Significant change and development, however, would wait until the twentieth century.

LITURGICAL DEVELOPMENT IN THE TWENTIETH CENTURY

In the first decade of the twentieth century, Pope Saint Pius X insisted on the importance of frequent, even daily, Communion. He decreed that children should receive their first Communion when they reached the age of reason. He encouraged the entire congregation to participate in the singing of Gregorian chant at the Eucharist. Not long afterward, the *Roman Missal* was translated into many vernacular languages for use by laity, allowing them to follow and understand the prayers of the Mass.

In his encyclical letter *Mediator Dei* in 1947, Pope Pius XII defined liturgy as the public worship of the Mystical Body of Christ in its Head and members. He taught that liturgy involves active participation by the members, the people as well as the priest. To encourage such participation, he recommended dialogue Masses. In the 1950s, building on the studies of German liturgical scholars, Pius XII revised the ceremonies of Holy Week according to ancient patterns of worship.

This set the stage for Pope John XXIII and the Second Vatican Council. In 1959 John XXIII announced his plans for an ecumenical council. The next year he issued a new set of rubrics for the Mass. In the first session of Vatican II in 1962, the bishops voted to approve the plan for a document on the liturgy. Discussion and rewriting of the document followed. The following year the bishops voted overwhelmingly in favor of the Constitution on the Sacred Liturgy, approving it by a margin of 2,147 to 4. A new era had begun.

THE CONSTITUTION
ON THE SACRED LITURGY

When the Second Vatican Council opened on October 11, 1962, I had just begun the final four years of my seminary training, the study of theology. Like most seminarians of the time, I followed the news of the council avidly, realizing its importance for those who would be ordained to the priesthood and for the whole Church. I was especially interested in reports about the document on liturgy. Would there be real changes in the celebration of the Eucharist and the other sacraments? Would there be more participation by the laity?

The Constitution on the Sacred Liturgy was promulgated on December 4, 1963, and answered these questions in the affirmative. The sacred liturgy is an action of Christ and of his body, the Church, a sacred action surpassing all others. This, therefore, calls for full and active participation on the part of all the members of the Church. To make this possible, the document called for a number of changes. The rites were to be simplified, the liturgical books revised, and a place made for languages other than Latin. There was to be a revision of the Church year, a wider use of the Scriptures, and a restoration of the homily. The prayers of the faithful, mentioned in early Church writings, were to be brought back. The use of concelebration and the administration of the Eucharist under both species were to be expanded.

IMPLEMENTATION OF THE DECREES OF VATICAN II

The Constitution on the Liturgy did not attempt to revise the rites of the Eucharist and other sacraments, but left this to the Holy Father, who was to employ the assistance of experts from various parts of the world and to consult the bishops. In 1964, Pope Paul VI set up a commission of bishops and a panel of experts who would carry out the actual work of restoring the liturgy. This began immediately, and in 1970 the pope promulgated the new *Roman Missal*. Over the next four years it was translated into vernacular languages. The official English edition was approved for use on November 13, 1973, with the changes envisioned by the council in place. The most obvious of these were three new eucharistic prayers and a revision of the traditional Roman eucharistic prayer, a transformed liturgical year with new emphasis on the importance of Sundays and the feasts of our Lord, and participation by the congregation in the ceremonies of the Mass.

A new book of readings, the *Lectionary for Mass*, offered a greatly expanded selection of the Scriptures (divided into a three-year cycle for Sundays and feasts, and a two-year cycle for weekdays). Anyone attending Mass daily would now hear a selection of the most important passages of the entire Bible. Sunday readings included a first reading usually selected from the Old Testament, a responsorial psalm, a second reading from the New Testament books, a Gospel verse, and a Gospel reading.

The new *Missal* was well received by most Catholics, especially where the changes in the Mass had been properly explained. I have celebrated Mass in many parts of the United States while preaching parish missions, and I have been impressed at the level of participation among congregations everywhere. The Catholic congregations of today are not perfect, of course, but I believe that if Saint Paul attended one of these Masses he would be delighted with the active, reverent involvement of the people, especially in comparison with that of the Christians of Corinth in New Testament times!

A second edition of the *Roman Missal* was approved by the pope in 1975. The English translation of this edition became available on March 1, 1985. This edition contained new eucharistic prayers for Masses with children and for Masses of reconciliation, as well as new ritual Masses and Masses in honor of saints. Other changes have been implemented with the approval of the Holy See. In 1977, the ancient practice of receiving holy Communion in the hand was restored. In 1994, girls and women were authorized to serve Mass. A new *Lectionary* with an expanded selection of readings was approved for the United States in 2001.

A third edition of the *Roman Missal* was promulgated by Pope John Paul II on March 18, 2002. The edition contains new Masses and prayers, and a revised set of rites for celebrating Mass, the *General Instruction of the Roman Missal*. The *General Instruction* was implemented in the United States in 2003. The English translation of the entire *Roman Missal* was approved by Rome and issued in August 2010, and it was announced that use of the new *Missal* would begin on the First Sunday of Advent, November 27, 2011. This translation is a faithful rendering of the original Latin. It makes allusions to the Bible more obvious and thereby links the *Roman Missal* more closely to the *Lectionary*. Its tone is more formal, more poetic, and more prayerful than earlier English translations.

The new *General Instruction of the Roman Missal* was in-tended to instruct Catholics, both clergy and laity, on the proper manner of celebrating the Eucharist. It will be used as the guide for our step-by-step explanation of the Mass in Chapter Three. A full discussion of the *Instruction* is not possible here, but information on the 2010 translation of the document may be found on the United States Conference of Catholic Bishops' website, usccb.org.

MY LORD AND MY GOD

My Aunt Lena never attended a theology school, but she knew that the essence of the Mass was Jesus himself, her Lord and God. Jesus gave himself under the form of bread and wine at the Last Supper, foreshadowing the gift of his body broken and his blood shed for us. When he rose from the dead, that gift took on a new meaning for his apostles and for all humanity, as Thomas recognized when he knelt before Jesus, his Lord and God. Jesus would be the Bread of Life for all people until the end of time.

The languages and ceremonies of the Mass have evolved through the centuries, but Jesus has remained the same—yester-day, today, and forever. The Mass he celebrated with those two disciples on the way to Emmaus, during which he explained the Scriptures to them and revealed himself in the breaking of the bread, has been the Mass of Justin, of Gregory the Great, of Pius V, and of every Catholic who celebrates the Eucharist today. The Mass is Christ, for Christ is "present in his word since it is he himself who speaks when the holy Scriptures are read in the Church.... He is also present in the Sacrifice of the Mass...especially in the Eucharistic species....and when the Church prays and sings" (*CCC* 1088).

QUESTIONS FOR DISCUSSION AND REFLECTION

If you could choose to attend Mass at any place and time (after the Ascension of Jesus), what place and time would you select? Why? Did you ever attend Mass before the Second Vatican Council? How many of the details of the celebration can you remember? If Saint Paul walked into your parish church during a Sunday Mass, what would he most approve of? What might he want improved? If Paul sat in the pew next to you, would you make any changes in the way you participate at Mass?

ACTIVITIES

Spend a few moments reflecting on the last paragraph of this chapter. Then place yourself in the presence of Jesus. Spend some time picturing yourself at the Last Supper with Jesus and the apostles, then with Jesus and the two disciples on the way to Emmaus. Next "attend" a Mass in the catacombs, then in a basilica in Rome after the Edict of Milan. Move on to a rustic country church during the time of Charlemagne and Alcuin. Then attend Mass at Notre Dame Cathedral in Paris, just after its construction. Visualize yourself at a Mass during the decadence of the fifteenth century and try to see Christ in the all-too-worldly priest who is leading the celebration, apparently with very little reverence. Then go to the first decade of the twentieth century and join the congregation as Pope Pius X celebrates a Solemn High Mass with music and beautiful ceremonies at Saint Peter's Basilica in Rome. Finally, place yourself in your own parish church and reflect on your participation at last weekend's Mass.

Someone has been present at all these Masses. Have you recognized Christ at each celebration?

Chapter Three

ATTENDING MASS:
STEP BY STEP

❦

W*hat does the Mass have in common with a baseball game, an orchestral concert, and a family reunion? Ritual.*

Ritual is a pattern for acting, a customary way of doing things, an established form for a human activity. Ritual is why baseball games and other sporting contests are so appealing and endlessly fascinating. Ritual is what helps concertgoers anticipate an evening at the hall and enjoy discussing the concert after it is over. Ritual is what draws members of a family to a park or parish center for a reunion, eager to meet and talk and share and feast.

Ritual is why so many new Catholics say, "What I like about the Mass is that I know what is going to happen next. And yet the Mass always seems different."

That's what is so great about ritual, and why ritual is so much a part of human existence. The ritual of a baseball game establishes a pattern where certain rules and expectations provide the framework for an unlimited number of possibilities. We gather at the ball park with friends and watch the teams take batting practice. When it's time for the game, the national anthem is sung, and the umpire shouts, "Play ball!" We know in advance that the game is scheduled to go nine innings, that in each inning a team will bat until it makes three outs. Each batter is allowed three strikes before being called out. If the pitcher can't get the ball into the strike zone, the batter walks to first base. If the ball is over the plate, the batter tries to hit it inside the foul lines where it won't be caught, or over the fence for a home run. Inside this basic pattern endless possibilities exist, such as double plays, stolen bases, and extra innings. During the game, fans in the stadium cheer, sing, chat, and consume large quantities of food and beverages. Those who understand the rules and the rituals of baseball can have a great time at the game. Those who don't know baseball, on the other hand, will likely experience much confusion.

People who attend orchestral concerts are familiar with their own rituals. They dress differently than baseball fans do. They might arrive at the concert hall early, take their seats, and listen to the musicians as they tune up. Just before it's time for the concert to begin, the concertmaster enters the stage to polite applause, signals the oboe for an A note, and the orchestra tunes up together. Then the conductor strides across the stage, acknowledges the welcoming applause, and takes his place on the podium. After a moment of silence the music begins. Customarily, the program begins with a short piece, then a longer solo composition, such as a concerto. The audience listens in silence, and claps only when each piece is completed. There is an intermission, when the orchestra takes a break while the audience files out to chat and perhaps enjoy wine and cheese or a dessert. Then the music resumes with a longer final piece, often a symphony. At the conclusion, the conductor turns around to the applause of the audience, bows, invites the orchestra to stand, and exits the stage. As the applause continues, he returns and singles out significant members of the orchestra before another exit. If the applause goes on, he might return to the stage again, bowing and acknowledging the entire orchestra. On rare occasions, an encore may follow. At its close, the audience leaves the hall.

The ritual of family reunions is less clearly defined than those of baseball games and concerts, but patterns are usually observed. Plans are made, a meeting place and date are arranged, and invitations are sent. On the designated day, relatives gather at the appointed place, bringing food and photos and keepsakes. Greetings are enthusiastic. Babies are given special attention as family resemblances are noted. Relatives share stories and photos while children play. Tables are covered with all kinds of food, a prayer is said, and dinner begins. After dinner family members may play card games or horseshoes and perhaps also gather for a singing session. As the day draws to an end, announcements might be made about plans for the next reunion. Belongings are gathered up, and relatives say good-bye and head for home.

The Mass too has its rituals. People come to church with certain expectations. They know the Mass has a definite structure, and within the structure many possibilities exist. The rules may not be as complex as those of baseball, but they do guide the conduct of those who are present. As at a concert, there are expectations about proper dress, times of silence, and ways of responding. Like a reunion, the Mass draws us to a definite location at a set time so that we might be with members of our family, listen to the family news, and share a meal.

But the rituals of the Mass surpass all other rituals because they find their origin in Jesus Christ. They are the product of two thousand years of human experience guided by the Holy Spirit. They put us in touch not just with a baseball team, a famous composer, or other people, but with almighty God. They allow us to join the events of our daily lives to the life, death, and Resurrection of Jesus.

The rituals of the Mass should never become routine or boring. While the general structure of the Mass remains the same, the readings and prayers change daily. We bring new experiences to each Mass, new hopes and dreams, new successes and failures, new blessings to count and new failings to regret.

In this chapter we will examine the rituals of the Mass and explain their meaning. First, we will discuss the environment of the Mass, the church building. A baseball game needs a field that has been properly prepared. A symphony requires a hall with good acoustics, a suitable seating area for the audience, and a stage where the orchestra is arranged. A family reunion needs an appropriate gathering spot. So, too, does the Mass require a particular environment and setting.

Then we will explain the actions of the Mass. This can be helpful to Catholics who are familiar with these rituals but may not always remember the reasons behind them. It should be helpful to those preparing to join the Church, and to members of other religions who attend Mass on occasion. In studying the environment, setting, and actions of the Mass, we will follow the *General Instruction of the Roman Missal*.

THE ENVIRONMENT

The Church. Catholic churches come in every size and shape, but whether we enter an imposing cathedral or a simple country church, we usually find a holy water font near the entrance. We dip our fingers into the water and make the Sign of the Cross as we pass the font. This blessed water reminds us of our baptism in the name of the Father, Son, and Holy Spirit. (Those who are not Catholic are welcome to make the Sign of the Cross and join in the other actions, prayers, and postures involved in Catholic worship, with the exception of receiving Communion.) The body of the church, where the congregation attends Mass, is called the *nave* (from the Latin word for "ship"). Somewhere in the nave is a place for the choir, which leads the community in song.

As we look around the church, we may notice statues of the

saints, visible signs that our prayers are joined to those of the saints as we worship God (see Rev 5:8). On the walls we see the Stations of the Cross, reminders of Christ's sufferings that are made present at every Mass. Stained-glass windows may portray scenes from the life of Jesus, saints, or images representing the sacraments and other signs of God's grace and presence.

Catholics genuflect (touch the right knee to the floor) or bow deeply before entering a pew as a sign of reverence to Jesus truly present in the Blessed Sacrament. Seated in the pew, we look toward the front of the church and see the *sanctuary* (from the Latin word for "holy"), where the altar is located. It is an altar of sacrifice, for here Christ's sacrificial death on Calvary is made present. It is also a table, where the Lord's Supper is prepared. The altar is covered with a white cloth (and may also be decorated with other cloths). Relics of saints are placed in or under the altar in a practice that goes back to the time when Mass was celebrated at the tombs of martyrs. On the altar or near it are candles and a cross, with the figure of Christ crucified. Flowers might be placed near the altar.

In the sanctuary is a pulpit, also called the *ambo* (from a Greek word signifying "an elevated place"), from which the Scriptures are proclaimed, the homily given, and the prayer of the faithful announced. Also located in the sanctuary is a chair for the priest who presides at Mass, and chairs for others who minister at the Eucharist.

The Blessed Sacrament is kept in a tabernacle (from a Latin word for "tent"), which is located in a part of the church that is noble, prominent, visible, decorated, and suitable for prayer. This place is marked by a lamp kept lighted to honor the presence of Christ, and may be in the sanctuary or in a chapel connected to the church and visible to the faithful.

The Vestments. The vestments worn by the priest are an important part of the environment at Mass. Their use goes back to the Old Testament when according to Exodus 28, God instructed Moses to provide Aaron and his sons with splendid vestments for worship. The vestments used today originated from garments worn in New Testament times as ordinary clothing. When fashions changed, they became distinctive signs of spiritual offices in the Church.

Under his other vestments the priest wears an *alb* (from the Latin word for "white"). It was the ankle-length tunic worn by Greeks and Romans in everyday life. The *stole* is a long narrow band of cloth worn around the neck over the alb. Its origin is uncertain; it may have been a symbol of authority. The *chasuble* is the outer vestment worn by the priest. It developed from a garment commonly worn in Greco-Roman times, a square or circular piece of cloth with a hole cut out in the middle. Its name came from the Latin word, *casula,* "little house," because it covered the whole figure. Today it is often beautifully designed and richly decorated.

The purpose of vestments is to show that the priest is present not on his own authority, but as a minister of Christ. The beauty of the vestments should raise our hearts and minds to God, and their colors have spiritual significance. White expresses joy, purity, and eternal life. Green, the color of growing things, symbolizes life and the vitality of faith, hope, and love. Purple and violet signify anticipation, purification, or penance. Red, the color of blood, symbolizes the supreme sacrifice of life given for others; it is also the color of fire and can represent the light and warmth of the Holy Spirit.

Jesus loved the world he entered through the Incarnation. He obviously believed that truth, beauty, and grace can be conveyed through created things. In Catholic worship, material things are used to "incarnate" spiritual realities, to signify the great gifts of God's love and our own efforts to respond with worship and praise. Church construction and appointments, vestments, and other elements of the Mass are meant to show that "all of us... seeing the glory of the Lord as though reflected in a mirror, are being transformed into the same image from one degree of glory to another" (2 Cor 3:18).

ATTENDING MASS: GATHERING TOGETHER

At a family reunion, relatives gather together so that they can be with one another. This differs from people attending a movie in a theater, where they assemble because it is convenient and economical for the show to be seen by a crowd. At Mass, as at reunions, we gather to be with members of our family. So it's fitting to greet others warmly as we enter the church's gathering space. It is appropriate also, after we take our places in the nave, to spend a few minutes greeting Jesus in prayer and speaking to the heavenly friends, the angels and saints, who worship with us.

The Mass begins with *introductory rites* and ends with *concluding rites*. In between are its two main parts, the *Liturgy of the Word* and the *Liturgy of the Eucharist*. All the parts are so joined that they form one single act of worship.

INTRODUCTORY RITES

Mass begins when the priest and ministers enter. The procession is usually led by a server carrying a crucifix, followed by candle bearers and a reader, who carries the book of the Gospels. On some occasions, a server may carry a thurible (censer), an incense burner suspended from a chain. Incense may be used during the service as a sign of reverence and of our desire that our prayers may rise up to God like incense. The congregation stands and joins in an entrance song that is meant both as praise of God and as an expression of unity.

The Greeting. The priest makes the Sign of the Cross, inviting us to join him. He then greets us with "The Lord be with you," an ancient biblical expression (Ruth 2:4; Lk 1:28), or with similar words. We respond, "And with your spirit." The priest, deacon, or lay minister may give a brief introduction to the Mass of the day.

The Penitential Rite. Next we are invited to call to mind our sins and failings as a way of becoming more worthy to worship God. After a pause, we join the priest in an act of sorrow. This includes some form of the threefold prayer "Lord, have mercy. Christ, have mercy. Lord, have mercy" and a prayer of forgiveness by the priest. (The *General Instruction of the Roman Missal* notes that this prayer lacks the efficacy of the sacrament of penance.)

On occasion, especially during the season of Easter, the blessing and sprinkling of holy water may take the place of the penitential rite.

> **MASS CONFUSION**
>
> *Marian, a devout lady and a loving mom, told me that when her children were small she was often praised for showing affection to her sometimes rambunctious brood by placing her arms around an unruly child. What others didn't realize was that she was also pinching an ear of the misbehaving child with the pressure only a mother could apply.*

The Gloria. Next, the *Gloria,* "Glory to God in the highest," is sung or said. This ancient hymn, whose opening words were sung by angels at Christ's birth, has been part of the Church's worship since the sixth century. During Advent it is omitted as a way of anticipating the joy of Christmas. It is omitted also during Lent, a season of penitence.

The Collect. The priest then invites the congregation to pray. We pause for a moment of silence to formulate our own petitions. Then the priest chants or recites the collect, so called because it is prayed for the people gathered (collected) together and because it collects all the intentions of the people into one. We respond, "Amen," a Hebrew word meaning, "Yes, we assent."

THE LITURGY OF THE WORD

At the Last Supper, Jesus led the apostles in the traditional readings and prayers. He then explained how the ceremonies would forever take on a new form and meaning through him. In the Liturgy of the Word, Jesus speaks to us through the Scriptures and invites us to ponder their significance in our lives.

The Liturgy of the Word includes readings from Scripture and a responsorial psalm after the first reading. The Gospel reading is followed by a homily. On Sundays and solemnities, the Creed is recited by the congregation. The Liturgy of the Word then concludes with the prayer of the faithful. A brief period of silence is appropriate after the readings and the homily. Silence and congregational responses allow us to honor God's word and make it our own.

The Readings and Responsorial Psalm. On Sundays and solemn feasts there are three readings. The first is usually from the Old Testament. At its conclusion the lector announces, "The word of the Lord." We respond, "Thanks be to God." The reading is followed by a period of silence, then by a responsorial psalm. The leader reads or sings a phrase. The congregation follows with the same phrase, which it repeats each time the leader recites a verse of the psalm. Next, a reading from the New Testament is proclaimed. Like the first reading, it is concluded with "The word of the Lord," and our response, "Thanks be to God."

The Gospel. After another pause, we rise for the gospel verse, which may be omitted if it is not sung. Outside Lent, the verse is introduced and closed with the Hebrew word *Alleluia,* meaning "Praise God." The Gospel itself is the high point of the Liturgy of the Word. A special book of the Gospels may be carried in at the beginning of Mass and placed on the altar. There it remains until it is taken to the ambo, perhaps with candles and incense, for the Gospel reading. The book may be incensed.

The Gospel is always read by a priest or deacon, who first asks God for the grace to proclaim the Word worthily. He then addresses the congregation, saying, "The Lord be with you." We respond, "And with your spirit." Next the priest or deacon signs himself on the forehead, lips, and heart while saying, "A reading from the holy Gospel according to...." We reply, "Glory to you, O Lord," signing ourselves in the same way, asking God to touch our minds to understand the Gospel, our lips to speak it reverently, and our hearts to love it. The priest or deacon may incense the Gospel book. At the conclusion of the Gospel he says, "The Gospel of the Lord" and kisses the book as a sign of reverence. We acclaim, "Praise to you, Lord Jesus Christ."

The Homily. Next comes the homily, an exposition of the readings that should relate the Scripture message to the everyday life of the congregation. Most experts suggest that the homily be about ten to fifteen minutes in length. Preparation for the homily is one of the most important tasks in the ministry of priests and deacons. A guideline often recommended is that homilists should spend an hour in preparation and prayer for each minute they speak.

The quality of a homily depends not only on the priest or deacon, however, but on the congregation as well. In the moments before and after the Gospel, members of the congregation should say a prayer asking the Holy Spirit to bless and guide the homilist. They should make the same effort to listen actively as they'd like the homilist to make in his preaching! An attitude of attentiveness during the homily can bring out the best in a preacher, while faces dull with resignation and boredom can discourage the most enthusiastic speaker. The more the members of a congregation try to listen actively to the homily, the more they will gain from it, and the more they will help the homilist.

MASS CONFUSION

When I was a small boy, I would often attend Mass with my dad in the choir loft of our country church. I remember being impressed with the piety of the men sitting in front of me as they nodded in agreement with what the priest said during his sermon...until I finally noticed how they kept on nodding long after Father stopped talking!

Most preachers welcome comments, suggestions, and positive criticisms about their homilies. In more than forty-five years as a homilist, I've been encouraged by compliments and spurred to better efforts by honest critiques. Above all, I've felt blessed when people assure me that I am in their prayers.

The Creed. The homily is followed by a time of silence, after which we rise to pray the Creed as a response to the readings and as our acknowledgment of the truths God has revealed. Either the Nicene Creed or the Apostles' Creed may be prayed at Mass on Sundays and Solemnities. The Nicene Creed was formulated in 325 at the Church Council of Nicea, a city in Northwest Turkey, and further developed at the Council of Constantinople in 381. The Apostles' Creed, which seems to have originated by the second century, proclaims what the apostles believed and taught.

As we pray the Creed, we should note that it has a threefold division based on the Trinity. The first part expresses our faith in God the Father, Creator of all things. The second honors the Son, Jesus Christ, who became human, died for our salvation, and rose to give us eternal life. The third turns our attention to the Holy Spirit, who makes us one in the Church. The last words of the Creed state our conviction that God's goodness and grace will bring us to eternal life.

At the heart of our faith is the belief that God became one of us in the Incarnation. To highlight this truth, we bow at the words "who was conceived by the Holy Spirit, born of the Virgin Mary." On the two feasts that especially celebrate the mystery of the Incarnation—the Annunciation on March 25 and Christmas on December 25—we genuflect.

The Prayer of the Faithful. The readings, homily, and Creed should make us more mindful of God's goodness and our responsibility to care for others. Therefore, we respond by offering prayers to God for the salvation of all. The pattern of prayer suggested in the *General Instruction of the Roman Missal* is a series of intercessions for the needs of the Church, for public authorities, for the salvation of the world, for those burdened by difficulties, and for the local community. Prayers related to the time, circumstances, or occasion may be added.

The priest begins with a brief introduction and invitation to pray. The petitions are given by a deacon or reader. We answer each petition with a response, such as "Lord, hear our prayer." The intercessions conclude with a prayer by the priest, and our response, "Amen." We then sit to await the Liturgy of the Eucharist.

THE LITURGY OF THE EUCHARIST

At the Last Supper, Jesus took bread and wine, gave thanks, and changed them into his Body and Blood, which he then presented to his apostles. At Mass, bread and wine are brought to the altar. In the eucharistic prayer, Jesus, through the priest, gives thanks and changes these elements into his Body and Blood, which we then receive.

The Preparation of the Gifts. The altar, the table of the Lord, is first prepared. Servers place on it the *Missal,* the corporal (a white cloth named from the Latin word, *corpus,* "body"), and a purificator (another cloth, used to wipe the chalice). At Sunday Masses the collection is taken up and then brought to the priest along with the bread and wine. These actions express that our offerings represent the gift of our lives, which we unite to the offering of Jesus. The bread and wine are placed on the altar, the collection in a suitable place in the sanctuary.

At this time, an offertory chant or hymn may be sung. The priest accepts the bread and wine at the altar. He holds up the paten (plate) containing the host and says a prayer praising God for this gift of bread. Next he pours wine into the chalice and adds a few drops of water. This practice probably dates back to ancient times, when water was mixed with strong wines to make them more drinkable. But the action has now taken on a symbolic meaning, the union of ourselves with Jesus, as indicated in the prayer said quietly by the priest: "By the mystery of this water and wine may we come to share in the divinity of Christ who humbled himself to share in our humanity." He then holds up the chalice with a prayer of praise to God.

If the offertory song has been concluded, the priest may say the prayers of praise aloud while holding up the paten and chalice. The congregation then responds, "Blessed be God for ever."

The priest may incense the gifts of bread and wine, the altar, and the crucifix. This symbolizes reverence for these sacred objects, as well as the desire that our offering rise up to God. A deacon or other minister may incense the priest to signify respect for his ministry and incense the people to acknowledge their dignity as baptized Christians.

Then the priest washes his hands at the side of the altar. In the early days of the Church, this washing had a practical purpose after the priest had received the gifts from the congregation. Now the washing of hands is symbolic, expressing a desire for interior purification, shown in the prayer the priest says quietly, "Wash me, O Lord, from my iniquity and cleanse me from my sin."

The Prayer Over the Offerings. The priest returns to the middle of the altar and addresses the congregation: "Pray, brothers and sisters, that my sacrifice and yours may be acceptable to God, the almighty Father." We rise and respond, "May the Lord accept the sacrifice at your hands for the praise and glory of his name, for our good and the good of all his holy Church." These few words express powerful reasons for being at Mass—to praise God, to seek God's blessings for ourselves, and to pray for the whole Church. The priest then prays over the offerings, asking God to bless them and us. We respond, "Amen."

The Eucharistic Prayer. Now begins the most solemn part of the Mass, the eucharistic prayer. A number of formulas for this prayer have been approved by the Church. These include Eucharistic Prayers I, II, III, and IV, two prayers of reconciliation, and three for Masses with children. All these prayers have, as the *General Instruction of the Roman Missal* points out, eight elements in common. Attentiveness to them can help us participate more meaningfully.

(1) *Thanksgiving* is the first, expressed primarily in the preface, of which there are many variations for different feasts and seasons. The preface begins with a dialogue, sung or recited, between priest and congregation: "The Lord be with you." "And with your spirit." "Lift up your hearts." "We lift them up to the Lord." "Let us give thanks to the Lord our God." "It is right and just."

The priest continues the preface, thanking God for salvation and for blessings relating to the feast or season. He invites the congregation to join the angels and saints in their praise of God.

(2) *Acclamation* is our response as we sing or recite the Holy, Holy, Holy, a prayer with roots in the Old Testament (see Isa 6:3) and the New (see Mt 21:9). The threefold repetition of *holy* is a form of the superlative: God is most holy! Ancient authors also saw it as praise for the three Persons of the Trinity. As we conclude the Holy, Holy, Holy we kneel, a posture of prayer used by Jesus himself (see Lk 22:41) and an expression of humble adoration (see Eph 3:14; Phil 2:10).

(3) *The Invocation of the Holy Spirit* seeks the intervention of the third Person of the Trinity so that the bread and wine may become the Body and Blood of Christ. We ask the Holy Spirit also to make us one in Christ.

(4) *The Institution Narrative and Consecration* recall the actions and words of Christ at the Last Supper. Christ now repeats the words of institution through the priest and so changes the bread and wine into his Body and Blood.

The priest invites us to express our belief in the miracle that Christ has just performed: "The mystery of faith." We respond with one of the approved formulas, such as "We proclaim your Death, O Lord, and profess your Resurrection until you come again."

(5) *Remembrance* comes next as the priest recalls the saving actions of Jesus, especially his passion, death, Resurrection, and Ascension.

(6) *Offering* the sacrifice of Christ is an essential part of our prayer. The priest presents to the Father the Victim of Calvary. This prayer allows each generation of believers to perpetuate on earth the greatest moment in history—Christ's gift of himself to the Father for the salvation of the world. In

this prayer we are given the privilege of offering ourselves in union with Christ and with all the members of the Church who participate in the Eucharist.

(7) *Intercessions* for the whole Church are included: for the pope, bishops, clergy, and all members of the Church on earth. We pray also for those who have died, and we remember the presence of the saints in heaven who pray for us.

(8) *The final doxology* (prayer of praise) brings the eucharistic prayer to a close with an expression of God's glory. The priest holds up the chalice and paten and sings or says: "Through him, and with him, and in him, O God, almighty Father, in the unity of the Holy Spirit, all glory and honor is yours, for ever and ever." We respond with an enthusiastic "Amen," by which we give our assent to the doxology and to the entire eucharistic prayer.

When we pray this Great Amen, we should give our assent to all the Gospel truths, to God's great acts of mercy, and to Christ's saving love, which rescued us from darkness and brought us into the light of this celebration. We should also realize that we echo the voices of countless Catholic Christians who, as Saint Justin testifies in the second century, have sung their "Amen" to these prayers.

The Lord's Prayer. The earliest liturgies mandated the praying of the Our Father. Gregory the Great noted how right it is for us to say over the Lord's Body and Blood the very prayer that Jesus taught us. Ancient writers and the *General Instruction of the Roman Missal* emphasize that in asking for our "daily bread," we should have in mind the daily bread of the Eucharist. They point out also the importance of asking for the forgiveness of our sins, so that we might worthily receive holy Communion.

The priest invites the congregation to join him in saying or singing the Lord's Prayer. At its conclusion, he adds the ancient prayer Deliver Us, which develops the last petition of the Our Father. The congregation responds with the doxology found in the *Didache*: "For the kingdom, the power and the glory are yours now and for ever."

The Rite of Peace. In some ancient liturgies, as we saw in the *Apologia* of Saint Justin, a kiss of peace was exchanged after the Liturgy of the Word (see also Rom 16:16). At the beginning of the fifth century, Pope Innocent I mandated that in the Roman rite the kiss of peace be given before Communion. This is fitting, for we should be at peace with one another before approaching the Lord's table (see Mt 5:24).

The priest recalls Christ's gift of peace at the Last Supper (see Jn 14:27) and prays for the peace of God's kingdom (another development of the Lord's Prayer). We respond, "Amen." The priest says, "The peace of the Lord be with you always," and we answer, "And with your spirit." Then the priest or deacon may add the invitation: "Let us offer each other the sign of peace."

This sign may be any appropriate greeting we are comfortable with, such as a handshake, an embrace (for family members and close friends), a nod, a smile, or a verbal greeting. The *General Instruction* says that the manner of this greeting is to be established by conferences of bishops in accordance with the culture and customs of the place, and soberly given to the people sitting nearest to them.

MASS CONFUSION

On the Feast of the Holy Family, I asked the congregation to offer one another a sign of peace. Four-year-old Mindy, who was a mascot for the grade school cheerleading squad, high-fived her mother and shouted, "We're gonna win." An older parishioner in the pew behind Mindy later remarked, "That girl has been to too many basketball games."

The Fraction. As we have seen, Christ's action of breaking bread at the Last Supper gave the Eucharist its name in New Testament times. Saint Paul provides an instruction on the rite: "The bread that we break, is it not a sharing in the body of Christ? Because there is one bread, we who are many are one body, for we all partake of the one bread" (1 Cor 10:16–17). The Eucharist joins us, therefore, not only to Jesus, but to one another.

We sing or pray the Lamb of God while the priest breaks the eucharistic bread. The words ("Lamb of God, you take away the sins of the world, have mercy on us") recall John the Baptist's testimony (see Jn 1:29) and may be repeated as long as necessary for the breaking of the bread. The closing petition is always "grant us peace."

After the breaking of the bread, the priest takes a small fragment of the host and places it in the chalice. This custom seems to have originated in Rome before the fifth century, when the pope would send particles of the eucharistic bread consecrated at his Mass to the various churches in Rome. A particle would be received by the priest at each church and placed in the chalice as a sign of unity with the pope. Elsewhere, the mingling of the host with the consecrated wine in the chalice seems to have been a reminder that Christ's Body and Blood, separated during his passion, were reunited at his Resurrection. Thus, the rite became a symbol of eternal life, as shown in the prayer said quietly by the priest: "May this mingling of the Body and Blood of our Lord Jesus Christ bring eternal life to us who receive it."

Communion. Then, to prepare himself to receive Communion, the priest says in a low voice one of the two prayers found in the *Missal*. The congregation at this time should also pray to receive Christ worthily. Next, the priest shows the congregation the sacred host, holding it above the chalice or the paten. He says: "Behold the Lamb of God, behold him who takes away the sins of the world. Blessed are those called to the supper of the Lamb" (see Jn 1:29; Rev 19:9). We join the priest in praying words adapted from the beautiful profession of faith and humility uttered by a Roman centurion: "Lord, I am not worthy that you should enter under my roof, but only say the word and my soul shall be healed" (see Mt 8:8).

While the priest receives the Eucharist, a Communion song may begin. Members of the congregation are encouraged to sing as an expression of their joy at receiving the Lord and of their desire for unity. As we approach the minister of the Eucharist, we should bow in reverence before the Real Presence, then receive the sacred host while standing. The minister says, "The Body of Christ." We respond, "Amen."

We may choose to receive the host on the tongue or in our hands. In the fourth century Saint Cyril of Jerusalem taught that those receiving Communion should make of their hands a throne to receive the King. Accordingly, we position our right hand under the left, let the minister place the host in the left hand, then step aside and using our right hand, receive Communion. (Those who are left handed may switch hands for this action.)

If Communion is given under both kinds, we next approach the minister of the cup. We bow again, and the minister hands us the cup with the words, "The Blood of Christ." We respond, "Amen," take the cup, drink of the Blood of Christ, and return the cup to the minister.

A point of clarification: We should not suppose that we receive only the Body of Christ when we consume the host, or that we receive only the Blood of Christ when we take the cup. Whether we receive Christ under the sign of bread or wine, we receive the whole Christ. Under ordinary circumstances, Communion under both signs is recommended, in imitation of the apostles at the Last Supper. But at times it is not possible or advisable for people to drink from the cup because of the size of the congregation or because of the danger of disease. Of course, those who wish to receive Communion under the sign of bread alone always have the right to do so.

When the distribution of Communion is complete, the priest and people spend some time praying privately. A hymn may be sung at this time. Then the priest says, "Let us pray." He rises with the people and says the prayer after Communion. We make the prayer our own by responding "Amen."

THE CONCLUDING RITES

As the Mass draws to a close, we prepare to return to daily life and work. Announcements may be made about parish activities or other matters. Then the priest addresses us again with the words, "The Lord be with you." We answer, "And with your spirit." The priest blesses us in the name of the Father, and of the Son, and of the Holy Spirit. We make the Sign of the Cross and respond, "Amen." On some occasions, a prayer over the people or a solemn form of benediction may precede the blessing. After the blessing, the priest or deacon says words of dismissal, such as: "Go forth, the Mass is ended." We reply, "Thanks be to God."

> ### MASS CONFUSION
> *I read about a family attending Mass one Sunday when the five children were restless and unruly. They quieted down at Communion, and the dad returned to his place, grateful for a few moments of peace. He covered his eyes and began his thanksgiving. His five-year-old son immediately put his hand on Dad's shoulder and whispered, "Don't cry, Daddy. We'll be going home soon."*

A hymn may be sung as the priest and ministers gather before the altar, bow, and process from the church. Before we follow we may wish to say prayers of gratitude to God for the graces of the Mass. Then we depart.

For many Catholics, the time after Mass is a good opportunity to visit with friends and parishioners and to speak to the priest and other ministers. Many parishes have greeting areas outside the nave where people gather. Christ brought us together and made us one as we received him in the Eucharist. It is fitting to express and enjoy this unity immediately after Mass and then strive to bring the love and peace of Christ to our home and our world.

THE SAME, YET DIFFERENT

The rituals of the Mass provide a framework for a variety of prayers, readings, and actions. But to really benefit from every Mass, we must remember that it is always Jesus' offering of his life, death, and Resurrection to the Father. We are privileged at every Mass to join the gift of our lives to the offering of Jesus. And what we bring to each Mass is never the same. Our hopes and plans for this week differ from those of last week. Our failures and our successes, our fears and our dreams, our joys and our sorrows, are constantly changing. We bring them to Mass, and Christ offers them to the Father, as our Eucharist becomes one with his.

QUESTIONS FOR DISCUSSION AND REFLECTION

This chapter mentions the rituals of baseball, concerts, and family reunions and then compares them to the Mass. Can you think of any other rituals that might be compared to those of the Mass?

Rob told me that at Mass he offers to God the problems he experiences at work, such as disagreements and misunderstandings. When he compares these experiences to the sufferings of Christ during his passion—made present in the Mass—his problems seem much smaller. Do you consciously try to fit the many aspects of your life into the ritual of the Mass? Into what part might you insert your failures? Your successes? Your fears? Your hopes?

Have you ever considered how your attitude might affect the homilist? Have you ever thanked the priest for a good homily? Have you ever offered suggestions or ideas for a homily? Have you prayed on a regular basis for the homilists at your parish?

ACTIVITIES

Technical terms exist that refer to various parts of the Mass; you might want to become familiar with them. You can impress your friends—or your pastor—by using these words at cocktail parties!

Anaphora: This term comes from a Greek word meaning "offering" and refers to the eucharistic prayer.

Anamnesis: A word referring to that part of the eucharistic prayer that recalls Christ's passion, death, Resurrection, and Ascension. It comes from a Greek word meaning "remembrance." In the liturgy it means more than just recalling something. Anamnesis means representing before God an event of the past so that it becomes present and operative.

Epiclesis: This comes from a Greek word meaning "to invoke." It designates that part of the eucharistic prayer that calls on the Holy Spirit to change our gifts of bread and wine into the Body and Blood of Christ. It forms part of the consecrating prayers and is said while the priest holds his hands outstretched over the offering. It also includes the prayer asking that those who receive the Eucharist may be sanctified.

Embolism: This comes from a Greek word meaning "insertion" and refers to the prayer inserted after, and developed from, the last words of the Lord's Prayer ("Deliver us, Lord, we pray, from every evil"). Note that *embolism* has a specific meaning in medicine: the sudden obstruction of a blood vessel by an abnormal particle circulating in the blood.

Chapter Four

PRAYING THE MASS

❧———❧

Did you hear that the pastor had an embolism at Mass this morning?"

"Oh my goodness. Did they call 911?"

"No. They just responded, 'For the kingdom, the power and the glory are yours now and for ever.'"

If the above (imaginary) conversation seems puzzling, you may want to review the Activities section at the end of Chapter Three!

It is important for us to know facts about the Mass, including technical terms that identify parts of the Mass, such as "embolism." But it is far more important to **pray the Mass.**

COMMUNION, COMMUNICATION

Prayer is communion, communication, with God. At Mass we achieve the greatest possible union with God this side of heaven. We step into the company of angels and saints who see God face to face. God speaks to us through the Scriptures. We respond by speaking to God our words of praise, thanks, repentance, and petition.

MEAL, SACRIFICE, MIRACLE

But the Mass goes beyond listening and speaking. The Mass is a meal at which we do what Jesus did with his apostles at the Last Supper: "Then he took a loaf of bread, and when he had given thanks, he broke it and gave it to them, saying, 'This is my body, which is given for you. Do this in remembrance of me.' And he did the same with the cup after supper, saying, 'This cup that is poured out for you is the new covenant in my blood'" (Lk 22:19–20).

The Mass is a sacrifice, one with the sacrificial death of Jesus on Calvary, where he was priest and victim. On Holy Thursday, Jesus identified the bread with his body to be given in death, and the cup of wine with his blood, to be "poured out for many for the forgiveness of sins" (Mt 26:28).

The Mass is a miracle, for it overcomes the barriers of space and time, letting us be present at the Last Supper, at Calvary, and at the empty tomb. It allows us to transcend the limits of this earthly life and to taste the delights of heaven.

THE CROSS

After Mass, little Paula, aged two, stood in the sanctuary awaiting her baby sister's baptism. She pointed at the crucifix over the altar and said, "There's Jesus." We could say the same of the Mass: "There's Jesus."

The Mass is full of meaning and rich in grace because it is Jesus Christ. How can we best realize its possibilities as we celebrate? One answer is to contemplate the crucifix, the image of Jesus hanging on the cross. The crucifix contains a summary of the many meanings of the Mass as well as a visual reminder of all that Jesus does for us at the Eucharist.

THE CRUCIFIX:
UNION WITH GOD

On Calvary the cross had both a vertical beam and a horizontal beam. As we attend Mass and gaze at the crucifix, we see Jesus with his arms outstretched on that horizontal beam. One arm is held out to embrace us: The Mass joins us to Jesus. One arm is held out to join us with those Jesus died to save: The Mass unites us to one another.

Christ's love for us and his desire to unite us to himself, to the Father, and to the Holy Spirit are beautifully expressed in his Last Supper discourse, found in the Gospel of John, chapters thirteen to seventeen. As John begins his description of the Last Supper, he connects this Passover meal to Christ's death on the cross. "Now before the festival of the Passover, Jesus knew that his hour had come to depart from this world and go to the Father. Having loved his own who were in the world, he loved them to the end" (Jn 13:1–2).

The reason Jesus gives his life, goes to the Father, loves us to the end, is to unite us to God. He goes to prepare a dwelling place for us so we can be where he is (see Jn 14:1–4). Jesus will die, but he will not leave us orphaned, for he will rise. "On that day," Jesus promises, "you will know that I am in my Father, and you in me, and I in you" (Jn 14:20). In his death and Resurrection, Jesus reveals himself as Savior, and when we accept his love, he and the Father will come and make their home with us (see Jn 14:21–23).

By his willingness to stretch out his arms and die on the cross, Jesus sends the Holy Spirit, the Advocate, to us: "It is to your advantage that I go away," he says, "for if I do not go away, the Advocate will not come to you; but if I go, I will send him to you" (Jn 16:7). This Advocate (Helper) will be with us, abiding in us forever (see Jn 14:17).

Jesus compares the union he establishes between himself and us to that of a vine and its branches. His life flows through us and enables us to bear fruit. "Abide in me as I abide in you," he says (Jn 15:4). He made this union a reality at the Last Supper by sharing with his apostles his own Body and Blood, to be sacrificed on the cross. At Mass, Jesus does the same for us.

Perhaps the most beautiful expression of how Jesus' love is shown on the cross is the simple language of friendship. "No one has greater love than this, to lay down one's life for one's friends. You are my friends" (Jn 15:13–14). So at every Mass, as we look upon the crucifix we should recall Christ's longing to draw us close to himself, close to the warmth of the love that radiates eternally from the heart of God the Father, Son, and Holy Spirit.

THE CRUCIFIX: UNION WITH OTHERS

The greatest commandment, Jesus tells us, is love of God. The second is love of neighbor. Jesus died to join us not only to God but also to one another (see Jn 11:51–52). At the Last Supper, he made this point clear by his actions as well as by his words. He performed the task of a slave and washed the feet of his apostles. Jesus wanted us to connect our efforts to love and serve others to his sacrificial death on the cross: "And during supper Jesus, knowing that the Father had given all things into his hands, and that he had come from God and was going to God, got up from the table...and began to wash the disciples' feet" (Jn 13:2–5). He performed this washing of the feet on the night before he died so that we would never forget those words that impel us to loving service: "So if I, your Lord and Teacher, have washed your feet, you also ought to wash one another's feet. For I have set you an example, that you also should do as I have done to you" (Jn 13:14–15).

The love that unites us to one another can be properly

measured only when we look upon the cross. "Just as I have loved you, you also should love one another" (Jn 13:34). There are times when we grow tired of trying to love others. We may be frustrated because they don't seem to appreciate our efforts. Husbands and wives, parents and children, may be worn down by the failings they see in one another. At such times Jesus asks us to look at him on the cross, arms outstretched, hands pierced by nails, and let his love be a source of strength for us. We must, if we wish to be his followers. "By this everyone will know that you are my disciples, if you have love for one another" (Jn 13:35).

When we are at Mass during such difficult times, we should draw hope and strength from the realization that Jesus knows our weakness and prays for us. He prayed for us at the Last Supper, and he prays for us at every Mass: "I ask not only on behalf of these [apostles], but also on behalf of those who will believe in me through their word, that they may all be one" (Jn 17:20–21). We should also draw courage from Jesus' incredible statement that the Father loves us as he loves Jesus (see Jn 17:23).

In the closing words of his prayer, Jesus said, "Righteous Father...I made your name known to them [disciples], and I will make it known, so that the love with which you have loved me may be in them, and I in them" (Jn 17:25–26). Jesus taught his followers in many ways that God is a loving Father. When he said, "I will make it known," he meant he would do this by his death and Resurrection.

We ask Jesus how much he loves us. He stretches out his arms to their fullest extent on the cross and says, "This much." The crucifix shows that his love for us is the infinite love of the Father for him. "God so loved the world that he gave his only Son" (Jn 3:16). His arms are opened wide on the cross so that risen and glorious, he might embrace us at every Mass, joining us to himself and to one another.

THE CRUCIFIX: ETERNAL LIFE

On Calvary, the upper part of the vertical beam of the cross pointed toward heaven. As Mary and John stood beneath the cross and looked up to Jesus, they could not help but see the clouds, signs in Scripture of God's presence and of the heavenly dwelling place of the just. The Mass, like the cross, directs our gaze to heaven, to God, and to the saints and angels in God's presence.

Jesus died to bring us to heaven. "And I, when I am lifted up from the earth," he promised, "will draw all people to myself" (Jn 12:32). The first to realize this blessing was one of the criminals who was crucified with Jesus. Raised beyond his own agony by the goodness of Jesus, he pleaded, "Jesus, remember me when you come into your kingdom." Jesus replied, "Truly I tell you, today you will be with me in Paradise" (Lk 23:42–43). We are given a similar promise when we receive the Lord during the Eucharist: "Those who eat my flesh and drink my blood have eternal life, and I will raise them up on the last day.…The one who eats this bread will live forever" (Jn 6:54, 58).

Heaven is the abode of those who have risen with Christ to eternal life. The cross directs our eyes to the residents of heaven— angels, saints, deceased relatives and friends.

Saints and angels were close to Jesus in his sufferings. On the Mount of Transfiguration, Moses and Elijah came to him. "They appeared in glory and were speaking of his departure, which he was about to accomplish at Jerusalem" (Lk 9:31). When Jesus endured such agony in the Garden of Gethsemane that his sweat became like blood, "an angel from heaven appeared to him and gave him strength" (Lk 22:43).

The link between the saints in heaven and Christ on the cross was shown when he took his last breath. "At that moment… the earth shook, and the rocks were split. The tombs also were opened, and many bodies of the saints who had fallen asleep were raised. After his resurrection they came out of the tombs and entered the holy city and appeared to many" (Mt 27:51–53).

Jesus' death and Resurrection unite us to those who have died, and them to us. We have seen that the Mass is like a family reunion. That reunion is not only with members of our parish family but also with those of our heavenly family. When we walk through the doors of the church for Mass, it should be with the realization that we will be spending time with our loved ones in heaven. We are never closer to them than when we celebrate Mass. So in each eucharistic prayer we call to mind Mary, the apostles, and all the saints, and pray for the grace to join them in heaven (CCC 1370).

We remember also those members of our family who are in purgatory. The Bible teaches that it is "holy and pious" to pray for the dead (see 2 Macc 12:45). Some people die neither cut off from God by serious sin nor perfectly free from the effects of sin. Such persons need further purification to achieve the holiness required to stand in God's presence, where "nothing unclean will enter" (Rev 21:27). So Catholics have always prayed for the dead, helping them on their journey to eternal bliss. At Mass, then, we ask that all who have died be brought into the light of God's presence (CCC 1371).

"By the Eucharistic celebration we already unite ourselves with the heavenly liturgy and anticipate eternal life, when God will be all in all" (CCC 1326).

THE CRUCIFIX: LAST SUPPER, CALVARY, CHRIST'S RESURRECTION

On Calvary the lower part of the vertical beam of the cross was sunk into the ground, rooted in the earth. This can remind us how the Mass is rooted in historical events: the Last Supper, Calvary, and the empty tomb of Easter. When we realize that the Mass allows us to become participants in those events, the Mass takes on new meaning.

Some years ago, five-year-old Meghan was spending a weekend with her family at their cabin on the Castor River in Southeast Missouri. On Sunday morning, as her dad drove the winding roads to church, Meghan became nauseated and began to cry. Her mother comforted her, "Don't cry, dear. You're just carsick. You'll feel better when we get to church." Sure enough, after arriving at the church and walking around the parking lot a bit, Meghan felt fine and went to Mass with the rest of the family. But the priest at that particular country church believed in long sermons, and as he preached on and on for more than thirty minutes, Meghan began to get restless. Finally, she leaned over to her mother, nudged her, and whispered, "Mommy, I think I'm getting churchsick!"

We'll never get churchsick, or sick of church, if we grasp the full meaning of the sacrament of the Eucharist. One method of entering into this meaning is to picture ourselves at the Last Supper, Calvary, and the Resurrection. We can do this in many ways. My own approach is to imagine myself at the Last Supper from the beginning of Mass through the Consecration, then at Calvary through the Lord's Prayer, and finally at the Resurrection until the end of Mass.

THE LAST SUPPER

As we enter the church, we can picture ourselves gathering with Jesus and the apostles in the Upper Room. Jesus intended that we should remember and relive the Last Supper, for he told his followers, "Do this in remembrance of me" (Lk 22:19).

The reality is that Jesus is present at each Mass. We have his assurance: "I am with you always, to the end of the age" (Mt 28:20). Jesus is not only present but he also continues his saving actions in the Eucharist. The Church came to its understanding of the Mass (and all the sacraments) by reflecting, under the guidance of the Holy Spirit, on the words of Jesus. Jesus said, "This is my body....Do this in remembrance of me" (Lk 22:19). Jesus must be present at every Mass, doing what he did at the Last Supper, for only his power can change bread into his Body.

Christ's saving actions cannot remain only in the past. If they did, they could have no effect on us. Since Christ is God, everything he did in his life on earth participates in the eternity of God and is always present to our time. It is brought into the here and now, this place, this moment, each time the Mass is celebrated. He now acts through the Eucharist, conveying to us the grace won by his life, death, and Resurrection. As the *Catechism of the Catholic Church* explains:

Christ is always present in his Church, especially in her liturgical celebrations. He is present in the Sacrifice of the Mass not only in the person of his minister, "the same now offering, through the ministry of priests, who formerly offered himself on the cross," but especially in the Eucharistic species....He is present in his word since it is he himself who speaks when the holy Scriptures are read in the Church. Lastly, he is present when the Church prays and sings, for he has promised "where two or three are gathered together in my name there am I in the midst of them" (CCC 1088, quoting Sacrosanctum concilium, Mt 18:20).

So when you come to Mass, use your imagination to see reality! Picture Jesus "disguising" himself as the priest, gathering the community together and leading the congregation in prayer, just as he gathered the apostles together and led them in prayer at the Last Supper. Hear Jesus proclaiming the Scriptures through the reader, song leader, and priest. Allow Jesus to speak to your heart through the words of the homilist, and remember that Jesus can use the most humble of instruments to touch hearts.

We who are Catholic need to appreciate better the treasure that is ours in the Scripture readings. Many converts to Catholicism have reported their surprise at learning how much of the Bible is read at every Mass. But we must be attentive to the readings. We must remember that Jesus is the reader at Mass. As the Scripture is proclaimed, we should try to grasp at least one passage that we can apply to our own life. And we ought to have a sense of the critical importance of Scripture. Someone has remarked that we should listen to the Bible readings at Mass with the same attention we'd pay to instructions on how to pack our own parachute!

As ushers begin the collection and receive our gifts, we remember that we are giving our lives to the Father along with Jesus at the Last Supper. When Jesus offered himself to the Father, we were part of that gift. He prayed to the Father for all who would ever believe in him, and identified us with himself (see Jn 17:20–24). Now at Mass we join each day of our life to the eternal offering of Jesus. This is expressed in the prayer said by the priest before he washes his hands: "With humble spirit and contrite heart may we be accepted by you, O Lord, and may our sacrifice in your sight this day be pleasing to you, Lord God."

The crucifix invites us in a special way to join our sufferings to Christ's. When we do this, we are truly one with Jesus. In the words of Saint Paul: "I have been crucified with Christ; and it is no longer I who live, but it is Christ who lives in me" (Gal 2:19). Even more, we can offer our sufferings along with Christ's for the salvation of others. In Colossians 1:24, Paul explains that he rejoices in his sufferings, because through them he is "completing what is lacking in Christ's afflictions for the sake of his body, that is, the church." Christ's sufferings and death were sufficient to redeem humankind, but Christ needs the suffering members of his Body to direct his redemptive love to the world. This is a mystery, but it is tied to the efficacy of love. Love joins us to God, and when we offer our sufferings in union with those of Jesus to God, we express our love for God and convey that love to others. Seldom can we come to church completely free of any kind of suffering. What an awesome privilege to be able to join our pain to that of Jesus for our good and the good of others!

During the eucharistic prayer and, above all, at the consecration, we should be aware of the presence of Jesus. He, through the priest, says the words that change the bread and wine into himself. As we hear those words, we might try to capture some of the awe the apostles must have felt at the Last Supper, and our sense of wonder should go beyond theirs. We know now what they could not have fully realized that Thursday night: Bread and wine are actually being changed into Jesus, the God who made the universe and who will reign over creation forever.

CALVARY

After the consecration, it is time to leave the Upper Room and stand at the foot of the cross. "For as often as you eat this bread and drink the cup, you proclaim the Lord's death until he comes" (1 Cor 11:26). We relate the separate consecration of bread and wine to the fact that Christ gave his body and shed his blood for us. The separate consecration makes his death sacramentally present. And so in the prayer said immediately after the consecration, we call to mind the sufferings and death of Jesus.

The words of the eucharistic prayer take on a special meaning when we pray with the knowledge that we are sacramentally present at Calvary. We might imagine standing next to Mary and put our arm around her as John, the beloved disciple, must have done. We can let her place her arm around us and help us unite ourselves to the sacrificial death of Jesus. As the prayers continue, we can think of the saints who have already been brought to heaven by the power of Christ's death. We can pray for the souls in purgatory who are now in the final stages of their journey to heaven. Our prayerful attitude can be a means by which the sacrificial death of Jesus pours strength and wisdom upon the pope, bishops, and all members of the Church.

Being at the cross with Mary will help us pray the words of the Our Father with new fervor. It might be difficult to mean "Thy will be done" when we are going through hard times. But if we look into the eyes of Jesus and recall his prayer in the garden, "not my will but yours be done" (Lk 22:42), it becomes easier to say and to mean "Thy will be done." It can be very hard to forgive enemies, asking God to "forgive us our trespasses as we forgive those who trespass against us." But when we hear Jesus calling out from the cross, "Father, forgive them; for they do not know what they are doing" (Lk 23:34), we cannot help but be moved to imitate him.

As the Last Supper anticipated Christ's death on the cross, so each celebration of the Eucharist recalls that death and makes it sacramentally, truly present. This eucharistic celebration does not mean that Christ dies again (see Heb 7:27) or that Mass repeats the death of Christ. Rather, Mass is "a sacrifice because it *re-presents* (makes present) the sacrifice of the cross, because it is its *memorial,* and because it *applies* its fruit" (CCC 1366).

The Eucharist is a miracle that rolls away the centuries and allows us to stand at the cross. "The cup of blessing that we bless, is it not a sharing in the blood of Christ? The bread that we break, is it not a sharing in the body of Christ?" (1 Cor 10:16). We become personally involved in the drama that took place at Calvary as surely as if we had been there two thousand years ago. The sacrifice of Jesus on the cross and the sacrifice of the Mass are one. "In the Eucharist the Church is as it were at the foot of the cross with Mary, united with the offering and intercession of Christ" (CCC 1370).

EASTER

After the Lord's Prayer, it is time for Easter. The Jesus we receive in holy Communion is the risen, glorified Lord. We will study the meaning of Christ's Real Presence in Chapter Five (see pp. 94–107). Here we will examine how the risen Jesus reveals himself at Mass and shares with us the joy of his Resurrection.

The connection between Easter and the Eucharist became clear on the evening of the day Jesus rose from the dead, and it is shown in the twenty-fourth chapter of the Gospel of Luke. Two disciples were on their way to the town of Emmaus, about seven miles from Jerusalem. They were discussing the events that had taken place the past few days, sadly recounting all that had happened, at which point Jesus joined them. Showing a great sense of humor, he concealed his identity from them and asked what they were talking about. They stopped in their tracks. "What?" questioned one of them, Cleopas by name, "Are you the only stranger in Jerusalem who doesn't know the things that have been going on?" Jesus (the very one to whom all these things had happened!) acted as though he had no idea. "What things?" he asked. They proceeded to tell him how Jesus had been arrested, condemned to death, and crucified. They added that some women had gone to the tomb that morning, found it empty, and said they'd seen angels who told them Jesus was alive.

The sadness that gripped these two disciples was evidence that they placed little trust in these reports. Further evidence may be found in Jesus' response: "How foolish you are, and how slow to believe the prophets!" He went on to explain all the prophecies in Scripture that had foretold his passion, death, and Resurrection. Then, as they neared Emmaus, Jesus once again showed his sense of humor, pretending to leave his two companions. But by now they were entranced with the words of this stranger and begged him not to go. "It's getting late," they said. "Come and stay with us. We'll have dinner for you!" So Jesus joined them at table. There he "took bread, blessed and broke it, and gave it to them" (Lk 24:30).

In the writings of Luke, these words are code for the Eucharist, and it was at the breaking of the bread that the two disciples recognized Jesus. He then vanished. Amazed and joyful, they recalled how their hearts had burned within them as Jesus explained the Scriptures. They rushed seven miles in the darkness back to Jerusalem. They told the apostles about their Eucharist, how Jesus had opened the Scriptures to them, and how they had recognized him in the breaking of the bread.

This encounter on the road to Emmaus was the first Mass celebrated after the Resurrection. The risen Lord proclaimed the Scriptures, the Liturgy of the Word, then made himself present in the breaking of the bread, the Liturgy of the Eucharist. Since that first Easter evening, Jesus has celebrated uncounted millions of Masses in every part of the world for twenty centuries. Each time he has opened the Scriptures to his followers and made himself truly present to them.

He continues to do so, each time we go to Mass.

DOWN TO EARTH

"All very well," we might say, "to talk of the risen Lord at Mass. But Mass at my parish doesn't seem like that to me. Babies are crying. People don't sing. The priest stutters. And kids are whispering to each other. I don't find Jesus in this!"

Or we might watch an elegantly produced worship service on television. A well-rehearsed choir sings magnificently. Athletes and movie stars give personal testimonies about how they've found Jesus. A fine sermon is preached. A huge crowd attends, responds with loud "Amens," and applauds frequently. As we watch, edified and entertained, we might feel embarrassed about the "unprofessional" manner in which Mass is celebrated at our own church.

Indeed, all of us know former Catholics who have left the Catholic Church for some denomination where they say they feel more welcome and have found Jesus.

A few observations...

First, Jesus didn't say, "I want you to find me in splendid productions that leave you feeling entertained." He said, "This is my body. Do this in memory of me." Any service that does not follow the pattern of the Last Supper is not the Eucharist that Jesus gave his Church.

Second, if we can't find Jesus in the imperfection of our parish church, in the imperfection of our world, we don't know Jesus. Those who can't find Jesus in a humble church would have walked past the manger at Bethlehem, looking for something more dignified and better smelling than a stable. Those who suppose that famous athletes and movie stars are the key to successful worship services would never have invited Jesus, who was looked down on by the high and mighty of his time (see Jn 1:46). Those who can't find Jesus among people who are less than perfect would have not found Jesus in the Upper Room on Holy Thursday in the company of his very imperfect apostles.

Third, these observations provide no excuse for mediocrity. We Catholics, precisely because we have the Real Presence, must celebrate Mass with enthusiasm. We must be a welcoming people. We must strive to express our faith in the way we pray and sing and attend to the readings. We must demonstrate our love of Jesus by the devotion with which we receive Communion and by the kindness we show others, in and out of church. We must do everything in our power to celebrate the Eucharist as well as possible.

But just as God is patient with us, so must we be patient with ourselves and one another. In the life of Jesus, in our lives, and in the Mass, we find a mix of the ordinary and the glorious, the lowly and the great. Paul expressed this well in the following magnificent hymn to Jesus. We would do well to reflect on these words of his each time we attend Mass, each time we look at the crucifix. They call us to recognize Jesus in his lowliness, and to worship him in his glory.

Let the same mind be in you that was in Christ Jesus, / who, though he was in the form of God, / did not regard equality with God / as something to be exploited, / but emptied himself, / taking the form of a slave, / being born in human likeness. / And being found in human form, / he humbled himself / and became obedient to the point of death— / even death on a cross. Therefore God also highly exalted him and gave him the name / that is above every name, / so that at the name of Jesus / every knee should bend, / in heaven and on earth and under the earth, / and every tongue should confess that Jesus Christ is Lord, / to the glory of God the Father (Phil 2:5–11).

QUESTIONS FOR
DISCUSSION AND REFLECTION

Many parishes place missalettes in the pews for the use of the congregation. Some people think that we should listen during the Liturgy of the Word, not read from the missalette. Others, pointing out that we better retain what we see as well as hear, think it is better to follow along in a missalette while the lector proclaims the reading. What is your opinion?

In this chapter it was suggested that we listen to the readings with the same attentiveness we'd give to instructions about how to pack our own parachute. Now imagine this: You have purchased a lottery ticket, hoping to win the prize of 175 million dollars. The six winning numbers are being read. The first five match those on your ticket. With what attention would you listen to the sixth? Can you think of other examples of attentiveness? In what ways are the Scripture readings far more important than parachute packing instructions or lottery tickets?

Can you call to mind three particular Masses where you were most touched by the love of Jesus? Why do these Masses stand out? Can you identify anything in them that might help you be more open to God's grace in the future?

ACTIVITIES

If you do not study and pray the Sunday Scripture readings in advance, consider the possibility. You can do this individually or with family or friends. The readings provide a variety of Scripture passages over a three-year cycle, allowing you to come into contact with most key passages of the Bible. Reflecting on the Sunday readings in advance will open your heart to the prompting of the Holy Spirit when they are proclaimed at Mass. You will listen to the homily more actively as you compare your ideas about the readings with those of the homilist.

Some parishes order extra missalettes which are then made available for individual or group study. You can purchase Sunday and daily missals at Catholic bookstores. Several companies offer subscriptions to missals giving all Mass prayers, readings for weekday and Sunday Masses, and a collection of prayers and reflections.

What is said in this chapter about participating in the Mass flows from the Church's teaching on the "priesthood of the faithful." The word *priest* comes from the Greek *presbyteros*, meaning "elder," and refers to someone authorized to perform sacred rites. In the Old Testament, consecrated priests from families tracing lineage to Aaron or Levi held a special place of leadership in worship. But there was also a priesthood of the people. The Jews were "a priestly kingdom and a holy nation" (Ex 19:6).

In the New Testament there is an ordained priesthood and a priesthood of the people: "But you are a chosen race, a royal priesthood, a holy nation, God's own people, in order that you may proclaim the mighty acts of him who called you out of darkness into his marvelous light" (1 Pt 2:9).

The *Catechism of the Catholic Church* explains: "The whole Church is a priestly people. Through Baptism all the faithful share in the priesthood of Christ. This participation is called the 'common priesthood of the faithful'" (CCC 1591). So Catholics come to Mass as a priestly people who offer themselves with Christ to God (see Rom 12:1).

Reflect on your place in the priesthood of the faithful. Consider how this should affect your participation as Mass makes present the Last Supper, Calvary, and Easter. (For an explanation of the priesthood, see pages 145–157 of *"We Believe..." A Survey of the Catholic Faith*, by Oscar Lukefahr, C.M., Liguori Publications, 1995.)

Chapter Five

Holy Communion

⤚✠⤜

Sister Briege McKenna was explaining the Real Presence to some children and said, "When you receive your first holy Communion, Jesus will come and live in your heart." A little girl responded with a big smile, "Oh, do you mean with his furniture and everything?"

Well, no furniture! But Jesus does come and live in our hearts when we receive holy Communion. We Catholics have always believed in the Real Presence. Our belief goes back to Jesus himself.

"This Is My Body, This Is My Blood"

At the Last Supper, Jesus took bread in his hands and said, "This is my body." He held up a cup of wine, gave thanks, and pronounced, "This is my blood." The Catholic Church believes that Jesus meant exactly what he said.

For Jews of Jesus' time, *body* meant the person, much as it does for us. If you point to yourself with the words, "This is my body," you are saying, "This is me." That is what Jesus meant: "This bread is my very self."

But Jesus' contemporaries viewed blood differently than we do. For us, blood is a word with technical, medical implications. We have blood types and blood drives. But for Jews, blood simply was life (see Lev 17:14). They knew if a soldier had his arm severed in battle, his blood would flow out on the ground and he would die. No blood, no life. Blood was the life of any person, identifiable with that person. So when Jesus said over the cup of wine, "This is my blood," he meant, "This is my life. This is my very self."

That is why we believe we receive Jesus whether we take the host or the cup or both. He changes bread and wine into himself to be present for people until the end of time. This miraculous event may seem too good to be true, and when Jesus first spoke about the Eucharist, even some of his followers would not believe.

THE EUCHARISTIC DISCOURSE
(JOHN 6)

In the Gospel of John, the Eucharist is introduced in the sixth chapter. First, Jesus multiplies loaves and fish, a miracle foreshadowing his ability to "multiply his presence" in the Eucharist. He walks on water, showing his divine power over nature, power capable of changing bread and wine into his body and blood. Then, after a crowd of people gathered to hear him speak, he urged them to seek food for eternity, himself.

"I am the living bread that came down from heaven," he proclaimed. "Whoever eats of this bread will live forever; and the bread that I will give for the life of the world is my flesh" (Jn 6:51). Immediately, some of his listeners objected, so Jesus declared: "Very truly, I tell you, unless you eat the flesh of the Son of Man and drink his blood, you have no life in you. Those who eat my flesh and drink my blood have eternal life, and I will raise them up on the last day; for my flesh is true food and my blood is true drink. Those who eat my flesh and drink my blood abide in me and I in them" (Jn 6:53–56).

These words shocked his followers. "This teaching is difficult," they grumbled. "Who can accept it?" Many "turned back and no longer went about with him" (Jn 6:60, 66). Jesus did not run after them shouting, "Don't go away. You misunderstood. I didn't mean that the bread is my body, but only that it represents my body. It's only a symbol!" Instead, he turned to his apostles and asked, "Do you also wish to go away?" Jesus was ready to lose all his disciples and begin his ministry over again if they would not believe in the Eucharist.

But Peter answered, "Lord, to whom can we go? You have the words of eternal life. We have come to believe and know that you are the Holy One of God" (Jn 6:68–69). Jesus did not water down his statements about the Eucharist, and Peter did not claim to understand them. He simply accepted them on the authority of Jesus, who had "the words of eternal life."

THE HOUSE OF BREAD

Even though the sixth chapter of John's Gospel is the first time during his ministry that we find Jesus teaching about the Eucharist, there are intimations of the Eucharist much earlier, in the descriptions of Jesus' birth.

A teacher wanted to explain the importance of prophecy, and she asked the children in her class, "Why was Jesus born in Bethlehem?" A little boy responded, "Because that's where his mother was." True! But why was Mary in Bethlehem? Because this was God's plan, revealed through the prophet Micah, who foretold that the Savior would be born there (see Mic 5:2; Mt 2:5–6). Why Bethlehem? One reason is the connection between Bethlehem and the Eucharist. Bethlehem means "House of Bread." Jesus is the Bread of Life (see Jn 6:35).

Another detail connecting Christ's birth and the Eucharist is found in Luke's Gospel. Mary placed Jesus in a manger, where shepherds worshiped him (see Lk 2:7, 12). A manger is, of course, a place for food, and Luke wanted to bring to our attention that Jesus would be our spiritual food.

OLD TESTAMENT FORESHADOWINGS

Christ's gift of the Eucharist was not granted in a vacuum. God had prepared the people of Israel to receive this gift. The most significant Old Testament background for the Eucharist is the Jewish Passover meal. As we saw in Chapter Two (p. 24), on the night the Israelites fled from slavery in Egypt, they were told to slaughter a lamb and smear its blood on the door post of their houses. This sign would cause the destroying angel to "pass over" their homes when he struck down the firstborn of the Egyptians. The Israelites ate the lamb with unleavened bread and bitter herbs. They were to repeat this meal each year to commemorate their deliverance from slavery (see Ex 12:1–28; Deut 16:1–8). It was at such a Passover meal that Jesus, the true Lamb of God, instituted the Eucharist. Just as the Passover lamb gave the Israelites nourishment for their flight from Egypt, so the Eucharist gives us spiritual nourishment for our journey through life.

After the Israelites escaped from Egypt, they were fed with manna, a miraculous food from heaven. The Gospel of John finds parallels between this manna and the Eucharist. Manna was bread for the Israelites' journey through the wilderness (see Ex 16), but the true bread from heaven is Jesus himself. "The bread of God," Jesus said, "is that which comes down from heaven and gives life to the world...I am the bread of life" (Jn 6:33–35). He added, "Your ancestors ate the manna in the wilderness, and they died. This is the bread that comes down from heaven, so that one may eat of it and not die. I am the living bread that came down from heaven" (Jn 6:49–51; see also 1 Cor 10:1–4).

Another Old Testament foreshadowing of the Eucharist is Melchizedek, the mysterious priest-king of Abraham's time, who offered a sacrifice of bread and wine (see Gen 14:18–20). Psalm 110:4 refers to this event in foretelling "a priest forever / according to the order of Melchizedek." The first Christians realized that this prophecy was fulfilled by Jesus, who offered the perfect sacrifice of bread and wine—himself—and who is a priest forever (see Heb 6:20).

THE TESTIMONY OF SAINT PAUL

Saint Paul was a devout Jew, familiar with the Hebrew Scriptures. He knew what Jesus had done at the Last Supper and what he had taught. Paul could place the life and teachings of Jesus in the context of the Old Testament passages that had foretold his coming. Paul was uniquely qualified to understand and explain the Eucharist.

And Paul leaves no doubt about his belief that bread and wine become the body and blood of Christ. He writes: "The cup of blessing that we bless, is it not a sharing in the blood of Christ? The bread that we break, is it not a sharing in the body of Christ?" (1 Cor 10:16). After describing the Lord's Supper (1 Cor 11:23–25) cited in Chapter Two (p. 31), Paul states bluntly, "Whoever, therefore, eats the bread or drinks the cup of the Lord in an unworthy manner will be answerable for the body and blood of the Lord. Examine yourselves, and only then eat of the bread and drink of the cup. For all who eat and drink without discerning the body, eat and drink judgment against themselves. For this reason many of you are weak and ill, and some have died" (1 Cor 11:27–30).

Clearly, Paul sees more than symbolism in the Eucharist. Those who receive the Eucharist unworthily, he says, are answerable for the body and blood of Christ. Because some of the

Corinthians receive Communion "without discerning the body" of Christ, they are judging themselves and receiving severe sentences of sickness and death.

TRANSUBSTANTIATION

The Church has reflected on Christ's words about the Eucharist ever since they were spoken. From the beginning, teachers proclaimed the Real Presence. We saw in Chapter Two how Saint Ignatius of Antioch, at the end of the first century, recognized the Eucharist as Jesus and warned against heretics who had left the Church because they would not profess "the Eucharist to be the flesh of our Savior Jesus Christ, which suffered for our sins, and which the Father, of his goodness, raised up again."

Around 150, Saint Justin the Martyr testified that Jesus Christ, "had both flesh and blood for our salvation." In the same way, the Eucharist is received "not as common bread and common drink" but as "the flesh and blood of that Jesus who was made flesh" (*First Apology,* Chapter 66; catholicforum.com/saints/stj29002.htm; accessed January 12, 2011).

These Christians believed that Jesus changed the bread and wine into his body and blood. It was not that Jesus was in, or with, the bread and wine, but that these substances were changed into the body and blood of Jesus. They were no longer bread and wine, but Jesus himself. Teachers like Saint Cyril of Jerusalem, who lived in the fourth century, noted that Jesus had changed water into wine at Cana. Certainly he could change wine into his blood. The bread and wine become the body and blood of Christ.

By the twelfth century, Christians were employing the term *transubstantiation* to express the miracle by which Christ changes bread and wine into himself. In 1215, the Fourth Lateran Council used this word in conciliar decrees. Then, to distinguish Catholic teaching from the heresies that arose in the sixteenth century, the

Council of Trent (1545–1563) defined Church doctrine on the Eucharist and on transubstantiation.

As explained by Trent, transubstantiation means that the substance, the essence, of the bread and wine becomes the substance of Christ's body and blood, while the species (appearances) of bread and wine remain. When we receive holy Communion, then, we truly receive the body, blood, soul, and divinity of the Lord Jesus Christ, under the appearance of bread and wine. The teaching of Trent, as well as a thorough presentation of Church doctrine on the Real Presence, can be found in the *Catechism of the Catholic Church*, 1373–1381.

BUT WHAT DOES IT MEAN?

Even though the Church's teaching that Jesus changes bread and wine into his body and blood is expressed in the *Catechism*, we may still have difficulty explaining it, especially to small children. Some children are frightened when they hear that we eat the body of Christ and drink his blood. What then?

When talking about Christ's Real Presence in the Eucharist to children preparing to receive their first holy Communion, I ask them what they believe about holy Communion. Invariably, they will say that holy Communion is Jesus. "Does this mean," I ask, "that Jesus shrinks himself up very small and then hides in the host?" "No," they'll call out, usually with laughter. "Or does it mean that Jesus sticks his finger with a pin and lets some of his blood drip into the chalice?" The answer is always a loud, unanimous "No!" The children know what holy Communion is not. So it's time to explain, in language they (and we adults) can understand, what holy Communion is.

I ask the children to recall pictures of themselves when they were infants. "You were a lot smaller then, weren't you? Were you still the same person you are today?" "Yes," they answer. Next

I invite them to imagine how big they will be in high school or college. "But will you still be the same person?" "Yes," they call back. "You see," I explain, "there is something that makes you who you are, and it doesn't depend on size or shape.

"That's how it was with Jesus. There was something that made him who he was as a tiny infant in the manger and as an adult dying on the cross. But Jesus is God, and he can do what we cannot. Jesus can take everything that makes him Jesus and fill the bread and wine with himself. The bread and wine then become Jesus.

"As you walk down the aisle at Communion time, everything that makes you who you are fills every part of you. Those are your hands and your eyes. Then you receive holy Communion. Jesus has filled that host with everything that makes him who he is. That means the host is Jesus. So when you receive Communion, Jesus fills you with everything that makes him who he is. Now your hands are the hands of Jesus. Your eyes are the eyes of Jesus. Remember his words, 'Those who eat my flesh and drink my blood abide in me, and I in them.' You go up to Communion alone. When you return, there are two. You and Jesus!"

(Note that the presence of Jesus in us after Communion differs from transubstantiation, where Jesus changes the bread into himself. It is no longer bread, but Jesus. In Communion, Jesus truly lives in us, but we do not lose our own identity. After Communion, our hands are the hands of Jesus, but they are our hands also.)

Next we consider the question: Why would Jesus want to be so close to you that he lives in you? The answer: You want to be close to those you love. You hug your parents and grandparents, and they hug you because they love you. Jesus loves you, and he wants to be close to you, so close that he lives in you and you in him. Holy Communion is his wonderful way of being close to all those who believe in him.

SACRAMENTAL PRESENCE

The sacramental presence of Jesus in holy Communion lasts, as the *Catechism* explains (C 1377), as long as the eucharistic species remain. After we receive Communion, this might be for ten or fifteen minutes. Therefore, it is important for us to be aware of this presence and to speak to Jesus in prayer after receiving.

What do we say to Jesus at this time? If there is a Communion hymn, we join in, paying special attention to the words and addressing them to Jesus, who now "abides" within us. During the period of silence after Communion, we should try to become more aware of the presence of Jesus. We make acts of faith, hope, and love. We talk to Jesus informally about whatever is going on in our lives. We place before him the needs of people who have asked prayers or who are experiencing difficulties of any kind.

Usually, the time of silence after Communion is too short for all we should say to Jesus, and it is fitting to spend a few minutes in prayer after Mass. Family members, as they get into the car, might want to remind one another that Jesus is riding home with them. They might discuss the readings or the homily. They can mention special prayer intentions. These responses to the reception of holy Communion could seem a bit artificial at first, but the presence of Jesus is real. A few moments of paying attention to him will be time well spent—and might keep us from getting too upset at the driver who cuts us off as we leave the parking lot!

The sacramental presence of Jesus is unique and powerful. Its duration is limited, but Jesus himself does not leave us after the sacramental presence fades. Rather, he comes to us in Communion to strengthen a bond of love and friendship that never ends.

"ABIDE IN ME"

Not long ago I was invited to a party celebrating Kristen's first holy Communion. After dinner, pictures were taken and gifts opened. Then the younger folks started a ball game in the back yard. Kristen, who loves to play softball and is very good at it, joined in—wearing jeans, a sweatshirt...and her Communion veil! As she ran the bases and dove after foul balls, I found myself thinking that her veil was a reminder of how Jesus had joined himself to Kristen that morning in holy Communion, not just for an hour of worship, but for every moment and event in her life, including ball games. No doubt Jesus was enjoying the game as much as Kristen!

In seeing the crucifix as a pattern for understanding the Mass, we considered that Jesus stretched out his arms on the cross to join us to himself and to one another. He had expressed his desire for union with us in his teachings at Capernaum and at the Last Supper, in anticipation of what he would teach by his death on the cross.

At Capernaum Jesus said, "Those who eat my flesh and drink my blood abide in me, and I in them" (Jn 6:56). Christ wants more than casual, distant relationships. He wants to be close to us, to live in us. At the Last Supper, he invited us into a friendship of intimacy and love (see Jn 15:15; 17:20–26). We can be together in many ways. A mother and her infant might be together in the same house. They are much closer when she holds her child in her arms. The Eucharist invites us to the closest possible intimacy with Jesus, a union both spiritual and physical. And after the sacramental presence, there is the presence of friendship: "I have called you friends" (Jn 15:15).

In John 15:4–5, Jesus uses the imagery of vine and branches to explain that we receive life from him. As a healthy branch gets its life from the vine, so we can thrive when we are sustained by the life of Christ. When Jesus handed the cup to his apostles with the words, "This is my blood," he was giving them a share in his life. Just as life flows from a vine to its branches, so Christ's life flows into us through the Eucharist (see Jn 15:1–5). Holy Communion, then, allows us to experience the presence of Jesus within us and to let his life flow through our veins.

The sacramental presence of Jesus after Communion should attune us to the indwelling of the Trinity. "Those who love me will keep my word," Jesus tells us, "and my Father will love them, and we will come to them and make our home with them" (Jn 14:23). The Holy Spirit lives within us, too, as Jesus testifies, for "he abides with you, and he will be in you" (Jn 14:17). This presence of the Trinity is not abstract or passive. The Father brought us into being and sustains us every moment with providential care. Jesus is our Savior and Friend, always near. The Holy Spirit is our Advocate, Helper, and Guide. That's great company to keep!

"WE...ARE ONE BODY"

Because Jesus abides in us, and we in him, we are joined to one another by the love and presence of Jesus. At the Last Supper, Jesus showed his love for his apostles by washing their feet, and then he told them they must wash one another's feet. They must be joined to one another by their love of Jesus and by their loving service to one another.

Christ's imagery of the vine and branches implies union, not only with Jesus but also with one another. His life flows through us, making us one body in him.

In his First Letter to the Corinthians, Paul emphasizes this aspect of the Eucharist. Those who receive Jesus are one because they receive the one Christ. Because the Eucharist is Christ and joins us to him, it also joins us to one another. "The cup of blessing that we bless, is it not a sharing in the blood of Christ? The bread that we break, is it not a sharing in the body of Christ? Because there is one bread, we who are many are one body, for we all partake of the one bread" (1 Cor 10:16–17).

Parents and children, husbands and wives, brothers and sisters, friends and parishioners—all need to be conscious that as we receive the one Lord, we are made one in him. This knowledge can build powerful bonds of love in families and communities. And when we allow Christ to make us one in love, we answer his prayer at the Last Supper: "As you, Father, are in me and I am in you, may they also be in us, so that the world may believe that you have sent me" (Jn 17:21).

In wonderful ways Jesus joins his disciples more closely to one another through the Eucharist. Michele told me that her husband, Jeff, attended Church with her every Sunday, even though he wasn't Catholic. When Michele approached the altar to receive holy Communion, she would carry their little daughter, Katherine, aged two, with her. One Sunday, as Michele was taking Katherine to Communion, the little girl exclaimed loudly, "But I want to go to Communion with Daddy!" Daddy took the hint. Two weeks later he entered the RCIA program at their parish. After his baptism at the Easter Vigil, little Katherine proudly sang "Alleluia!" When Michele told Katherine, now six years old, that she had shared this incident with me, her response was, "...(sigh) My life is so good!"

"My Life Is So Good"

Jesus can make the lives of every one of us "so good," if we accept the Eucharist with hearts open to his love and to the love of others. But Jesus makes this miraculous gift so easily available to us that we might take it for granted.

Scott Hahn, once an anti-Catholic Protestant minister, converted to Catholicism in 1986 and now teaches theology at

Franciscan University in Steubenville, Ohio. He says that when he became convinced from a study of Scripture that Jesus really does change bread and wine into himself, he could hardly wait to receive his first holy Communion. But it wasn't long before he noticed that some Catholics fail to show proper appreciation for the Eucharist. Some leave church before Mass is ended. Some don't attend Mass when they should. Scott suggests that we consider the following scenario...

What if Jesus at the Last Supper had taken the bread and said, "This is one million dollars," and transformed the bread into that sum? What if at Mass the priest would say "One million dollars" instead of "The Body of Christ," and Christ changed the host into one million dollars as each person came forward?

If this were so, Catholics would never miss Sunday Mass. They'd go every day! And if they had to be free of mortal sin for the miracle to occur, lines for confession at every Church in the world would stretch around the block.

That's the scenario. Well, let's be honest. Most of us could use a million dollars. But I guarantee that when you get to heaven, you will say to Jesus, "Thank you for changing the host, not just into a million dollars, but into yourself. Who needs a million dollars here in heaven, where the streets are paved with gold? But it was your Body, Lord, that got me here. You are the living bread, and all who eat this bread live forever!"

I shared these ideas with a priest friend, Father Charles Shelby. He remarked that one Sunday at Mass, without explanation, we should say at Communion each time we hold out the host, "One million dollars." Then we should process out of church, again without any explanation. People would come to us after Mass and exclaim, "Father, do you realize what you did? Instead of saying, 'The Body of Christ,' you said, 'One million dollars.'" We should then reply, "Oh, I'm sorry. I underestimated the value of the host."

How very true! The Eucharist is far more precious than any amount of money. The Eucharist is Jesus, who was born at Bethlehem, worked miracles, died on the cross, rose from the grave. At Communion we are united to the God who made the universe, who guides creation with mighty power, and who will judge us at the moment of death.

Can we possibly absorb the full meaning of this? Can we ever respond adequately? Nothing on earth is greater than being in the presence of Jesus. It is possible to forget this, however, and we need often to give ourselves a reality check.

People will go to great lengths to see a famous politician, to get an autograph from a celebrity, or to attend a concert by a popular singer. On such occasions people shout, scream, even faint from excitement. But at every Mass, Jesus Christ, the greatest human being who ever lived, "our Lord and God," is present. He is here, not as an aloof dignitary, but as One who enters our hearts and gives us a personal audience, not just an autograph. He doesn't want us to faint, but he certainly wants us to recognize him and to focus our minds and hearts on him. Why? Not because Jesus needs our acclaim, but because we need him for life itself. "Unless you eat the flesh of the Son of Man and drink his blood, you have no life in you" (Jn 6:53).

May we at every Mass see Jesus with eyes of faith, receive him with love, and carry his loving presence into our homes, neighborhoods, workplaces, schools—and ball games!

QUESTIONS FOR
DISCUSSION AND REFLECTION

Before Jesus instituted the Eucharist, he washed the feet of his apostles. He then taught us to serve one another in imitation of him. Do we try to imitate the humility and love of Christ? Do we appreciate the magnificent gift Jesus made at the Last Supper, the gift of himself? Do we realize that, as the *Catechism* teaches (CCC 1348), it is Jesus who gathers us together at every Mass, leads us in prayer, proclaims the Scriptures to us, and nourishes us with his body and blood? Do we frequently visit Jesus in the Blessed Sacrament and spend time with him?

The devotion of faithful Catholics to the Eucharist has drawn many to the Church. Sadly, a lack of respect and reverence for the Eucharist has caused some people to walk away from the Church. Does our attitude to the Mass and Eucharist attract people to the Catholic Faith?

I've been occasionally amazed at misunderstandings of the Eucharist among some Catholics. An elderly gentleman, Catholic all his life, stated on his deathbed to Father John that he longed to receive the Body of Christ as priests do. Asked what he meant, the old man explained that he thought the priest's words at Mass, "This is my Body," applied only to the host in the priest's hands and that the other hosts on the altar were only symbols! When Father John explained that the words of consecration change all the hosts into Christ's Body, the old man broke down crying and asked to receive Communion one more time. Tears streaming down his face, he took Communion, finally aware that he was receiving Jesus.

Once as I was distributing Communion and running low on hosts, I began breaking the hosts into smaller particles. A server asked if he should get some more hosts from the sacristy, apparently not realizing the difference between consecrated and unconsecrated hosts! Have you ever heard of misunderstandings such as these? What do they show about the need for careful catechesis?

ACTIVITIES

Read Chapters 13 to 17 of John's Gospel prayerfully. Try to picture yourself with Jesus and the apostles as he speaks these words, and realize that he is speaking them to you, here and now. Pray about those passages which touch your heart or apply to your life.

Pray the Fifth Luminous Mystery of the Rosary, "The Institution of the Eucharist." You might use the following reflections for meditation as you say the vocal prayers…

"Blessed art thou among women, and blessed is the fruit of thy womb, Jesus." You've prayed these words of the New Testament thousands of times, and you find yourself thinking, "How wonderful for Mary to have Jesus dwelling in her womb. For nine months, Mary held within her the Creator of the universe!"

As you continue to pray, hear Mary speaking to your soul. "Yes," she whispers, "it was a glorious privilege to hold God in my womb. But never forget that my Son loves you so much that he wanted to live in you as well. So he gave you the Eucharist."

Your thoughts turn to Jesus at the Last Supper. You join him and his apostles at this solemn meal recalling the Jewish Passover from slavery to freedom. Jesus holds bread in his hands and says, "Take and eat; this is my body, given for you." You receive the body of Christ with reverence, marveling that Jesus lives in you, and you in him (see Jn 6:56). Then Jesus takes a cup of wine. "This is the cup of my blood, the blood of the New Covenant, blood to be shed for you and all the world. Drink it, now and until the end of time, in remembrance of me." You take the cup and receive the life of Christ, life that now becomes your life as well (see Jn 6:54).

Now you realize something more clearly than ever. You really are present at the Last Supper and really do hold Christ within you each time you attend Mass. You end this mystery with awe-filled praise: "Glory be to the Father, and to the Son, and to the Holy Spirit."

Chapter Six

FREQUENTLY
ASKED QUESTIONS

〜※〜

Perhaps the most frequently asked question about Mass is, "Mom, Dad, why do I have to go to Mass?" Hopefully, we have provided answers in Chapter One, but it is worth noting that when children ask this question, they are really asking, "Mom, Dad, why do **you** go to Mass?" Often the best answer to a question about the Mass is personal witness, and any answer can be enhanced by the sharing of one's own experience. A person might argue about whether or not God's commandments include Sunday worship, but no one can argue with your own personal witness and experience.

So if your children ask, "Why do I have to go to Mass?" you might respond, "Let's take a moment and talk about that. But I want to begin by saying that Mass has been a great blessing in my life. Jesus has touched me in so many ways through Scripture, holy Communion, and our Catholic community that I can't imagine life without Mass. I want you to have such blessings." Then you could go on to discuss the reasons for going to Mass explained in Chapter One of this book.

The questions in this chapter are indeed "Frequently Asked Questions." Most have been asked by students of the Catholic Home Study Program I direct, by children in religion classes, or by members of adult religious education classes and RCIA programs.

Some of these questions may be ones you would like to ask. Others may be asked of you by friends who want to know more about Catholicism and the Eucharist. Still others may be placed by acquaintances who are hostile to Catholicism. I hope that the answers you find here will be helpful in each situation, but remember that each answer can be made more effective by bringing in your own personal experience.

Q Most Protestant churches use the cross, not the crucifix, as a symbol. Why do Catholics portray Christ on the cross in their churches even though he is risen?

A Christ has risen, but he endured terrible sufferings on the cross for us, and we should never forget the love he showed in doing so. This was the attitude of Saint Paul, who proclaimed "Christ crucified" (see 1 Cor 1:23). He added: "For I decided to know nothing among you except Jesus Christ, and him crucified" (1 Cor 2:2). He told the Galatians, "It was before your eyes that Jesus Christ was publicly exhibited as crucified!" (Gal 3:1). The Galatians were not among those at Christ's crucifixion, so Paul had to have placed this image in their minds by his preaching or even by some visual representation. Paul proclaims: "May I never boast of anything except the cross of our Lord Jesus Christ, by which the world has been crucified to me, and I to the world" (Gal 6:14). Clearly, Paul did not want us to forget Christ's death and consider only his Resurrection.

Some Christians who object to the image of Christ on the cross don't hesitate to show him in the manger at Christmas. It is good for us to remember Christ as a little child, even though he is no longer a little child, because this reminds us of how completely he shares our humanity. It is also good for us to remember Christ on the cross. This does not deny his Resurrection. It emphasizes his love, for he said, "No one has greater love than this, to lay down one's life for one's friends" (Jn 15:13).

The crucifix also invites us to unite our sufferings to those of Jesus. We all experience unavoidable pain and suffering. The crucifix reminds us of Jesus' words that we must take up our cross each day and follow him (see Lk 9:23). Following Christ imparts to suffering a value that is eternal. When we join our sufferings to those of Christ we are literally united to his own life. In the words of Saint Paul, "I have been crucified with Christ; and it is no longer I who live, but it is Christ who lives in me" (Gal 2:19).

For these reasons, before Mass or any time, we can make our own the beautiful prayer for the blessing of a cross from the Church's *Book of Blessings* (#1250): "Father, we honor this cross as the sign of our redemption. May we reap the harvest of salvation planted in pain by Christ Jesus. May our sins be nailed to his cross, the power of life released, pride conquered, and weakness turned to strength. May the cross be our comfort in trouble, our refuge in the face of danger, our safeguard on life's journey, until you welcome us to our heavenly home."

Q I have some friends who ask me why Catholics worship statues. They say the Bible forbids the making of images. Why do we Catholics have statues of saints in our churches?

A Catholics do not worship statues, and they do not worship saints. Worship and adoration are terms that refer to the act of acknowledging God as the Supreme Being. Catholics worship and adore God alone. Catholics do honor the saints as great followers of Jesus, and they do have statues of the saints. This is not prohibited in the Bible, but encouraged.

God gave Moses the commandment: "I am the LORD your God....You shall not make for yourself an idol..." (Ex 20:2, 4).

God forbade the making of *idols* (representations of false gods), not of all statues and images. Exodus 25:18–22 relates how God commanded Moses to make two cherubim (carvings of angelic guardians) and to place them above the Ark of the Covenant. Numbers 21:4–9 says that when the Israelites sinned against God and were being tormented by poisonous serpents, God told Moses to make an image of a snake and put it on a pole. All who looked at the snake would be healed. Images of cherubim, palm trees, and flowers, and carvings of oxen, lions, and cherubim were placed in Solomon's Temple in Jerusalem (see 1 Kings 6:23–30; 7:23–29). The Bible says God was pleased with the Temple and all its details, and dwelt in that Temple (see 1 Kings 8).

God likes statues! So should we. But we do not pray to statues but to the saints they represent. Statues help us remember the saints, whom we honor and invoke as the Bible commands: "Remember your leaders, those who spoke the word of God to you; consider the outcome of their way of life, and imitate their faith" (Heb 13:7). Statues remind us that saints watch over us as a great "cloud of witnesses" (Heb 12:1). When we pray on earth, they offer our prayers like incense to God in heaven (see Rev 5:8). When we worship God here, we join the praises they sing to God in heaven (see Rev 5:13). Statues of the saints remind us that we are part of a larger family, the communion of saints, those who are joined to Jesus here on earth and on the other side of death.

Q What is the meaning of the votive candles in various parts of the church?

A Votive candles are a way of expressing our prayers in visible form, showing our desire to pray always (see Lk 18:1) and continuing our petitions even after we leave church. Such candles may be lit before the Blessed Sacrament or before statues of the Blessed Mother and the saints. If placed before statues of Mary and the saints, they demonstrate our wish that the saints pray for us. If placed before Jesus in the Blessed Sacrament, they symbolize our worship of him. All candles represent our belief in Jesus, the Light of the world (see Jn 8:12), and they remind us that the saints and believers of every age have put their trust in Jesus.

Q I've been in some churches that have altars along the side of the nave or at the side of the sanctuary. Why these altars?

A Before concelebration became a common practice after the Second Vatican Council, churches that were served by large numbers of priests (for example, at a Catholic university or seminary) might have many altars because the priests would celebrate their daily Mass at these altars. Usually, they would be assisted by a server, and a small group of people might also attend. Such altars are seldom used today, but they serve as shrines that honor saints or Jesus under one of his titles, such as "Christ the King."

Q Our church bulletin has a section listing "Mass Intentions," and the priest may announce that a Mass is being said for a particular intention. What does this mean?

A A priest may offer Mass for a special intention, such as good weather, or for a person, living or deceased, Catholic or non-Catholic. Anytime a priest celebrates Mass for a particular intention, or when we offer our participation at Mass for a special intention, we offer the most powerful prayer possible, and Christ's love will certainly touch those for whom we offer the Mass. It has been the custom in the United States and many other places to make a small offering for the support of the church when requesting Masses for a specific intention. This offering, or stipend, (not required if the person requesting the Mass cannot afford it) becomes part of one's prayer, just as any almsgiving can be offered to God as prayer.

Most often, Masses are offered for the deceased. Even in Old Testament times great Jewish leaders prayed for the dead and sent donations to the Temple in Jerusalem so that sacrifices might be offered for them. Scripture praises this practice as "holy and pious" (2 Macc 12:45), and there is no greater sacrifice possible than that of the Mass.

Why pray for the dead or have Masses offered for them? Some people die neither cut off from God by serious sin nor perfectly free from the effects of sin. Such persons need further purification to achieve the holiness required to stand in God's presence, where "nothing unclean will enter" (Rev 21:27).

We do not know who might need purgatory, and since those in purgatory are beyond earth's space and time, it is not possible to know how long anyone might be there. God is not limited by time, and God can take our prayers of a lifetime and apply them to the needs of loved ones at the time of their death. We may pray or have Masses offered for our beloved dead as long as we wish. If those we pray for are in heaven, we can be sure that God applies the prayers to someone else who does need them.

When Masses are offered for someone living on earth, the benefits will depend in part on how open that person is to God's grace. We do our part by praying and having the Masses offered, then leave the matter in God's providential care.

Q A friend tells me we no longer need to go to the sacrament of penance because the penitential rite at the beginning of Mass has the same effect as confession. Is this true?

A The *General Instruction of the Roman Missal* notes that the penitential rite lacks the efficacy of the sacrament of penance. The *Catechism of the Catholic Church* states that we must confess all mortal sins in the sacrament of penance. Anyone who is aware of having committed mortal sin must receive the sacrament before going to Communion unless there is a grave reason for receiving Communion and there is no possibility of going to confession (CCC 1456–57).

The real issue is not how often we **must** go to the sacrament of penance, but how often we **should** go to meet Christ in this beautiful sacrament and receive its special graces.

Q My grandmother talks about the "Easter duty." What does this mean?

A The Easter duty refers to the obligation Catholics have of receiving holy Communion at least during the Easter season. This is listed as the third precept of the Church in the *Catechism of the Catholic Church* (CCC 2042; *Code of Canon Law*, 920). In the United States the time for fulfilling the Easter duty has been extended from the First Sunday of Lent to Trinity Sunday. Since Catholics are obliged to confess any grave sins before receiving holy Communion, the Easter duty would also include confession for those in grave sin (CCC 1457; 2042; *Code of Canon Law*, 989). Obviously, these laws establish the bare minimum for being a practicing Catholic. We ought to receive Communion as frequently as possible and go to the sacrament of penance often. (The entire *Code of Canon Law* may be found at vatican.va/archive/ENG1104/_INDEX.HTM; accessed January 12, 2011.)

Q May Roman Catholics attend Eastern-rite Masses and receive holy Communion at these Masses?

A Eastern-rite Catholic churches in union with Rome have the same creed and the same seven sacraments as the Roman Catholic Church. They accept the authority of the pope as we do. They have their own traditional style of living Christianity, with a cultural heritage different from ours. They have different rituals in celebrating the Mass and sacraments. Incense, processions, and singing are more frequent than in the Latin rite, and the language may be different. We are free to go to such Churches and to receive the sacraments of penance and Eucharist there because they are as fully Catholic as we are. However, children are to be baptized in the rite of their parents. Adults may transfer to another rite only with the permission of the Apostolic See or when marrying a person of another rite.

The Eastern Catholic churches in union with Rome are divided into five rites, which include twenty-one church divisions or jurisdictions in various countries or areas. They are as follows: **Alexandrian rite** (Coptic, Ethiopian); **Antiochene rite** (Malankar, Maronite, Syrian); **Armenian rite** (Armenian); **Byzantine rite** (Albanian, Belarussian, Bulgarian, Croatian, Greek, Hungarian, Italo-Albanian, Melkite, Romanian, Russian, Ruthenian, Slovak, Ukrainian); **Chaldean rite** (Chaldean, Syro-Malabar).

Eastern-rite Catholic churches should be distinguished from Eastern Orthodox churches, which have separated from Rome and do not accept the authority of the pope. Orthodox churches have a valid sacramental system and ordained ministry, and Catholic canon law states that properly disposed orthodox Catholics who request sacraments in Roman Catholic churches may receive them (Canon 844). Because of the unity of ministry and sacraments among Catholics and Eastern Orthodox churches, Catholics may, in cases of necessity, receive the sacraments in Eastern Orthodox churches. Before doing this, a Catholic should check with the pastor of the Orthodox church. Our law permits a Catholic to receive the sacraments in an Orthodox church, but this may be forbidden by a particular Orthodox church community. If allowed, Catholics should observe all the Orthodox rules about fasting and the manner of receiving Communion.

Q How is the date for Easter determined?

A The date of Easter recalls the Resurrection of Jesus, on the third day after his crucifixion, which occurred on or near Passover, the fourteenth of the month of Nisan, according to the Jewish calendar. Over the centuries, there has been much disagreement about how to decide the date of celebration, complicated by the change from the Jewish lunar calendar to our solar calendar. The Council of Nicea in A.D. 325 placed Easter on the Sunday following the first full moon after the vernal equinox, the day in Spring when we have a twelve-hour day and twelve-hour night (March 20). After this date, daytime exceeds nighttime, and this emphasizes the fact that the risen Christ is the Light of the world. Easter may be as early as March 22 or as late as April 25. The reason it was set according to a seasonal pattern rather than on a specific date was to assure that the celebration of Easter would always be on a Sunday, the day Christ rose from the dead.

Q A friend told me that by Church law only men can be acolytes. Our parish allows girls to serve Mass. Is this allowed?

A The National Conference of Catholic Bishops in 1994 mandated the following: Although institution into the ministry of acolyte is reserved to lay men, the diocesan bishop may permit the liturgical functions of the instituted acolyte to be carried out by altar servers, men and women, boys and girls. So while only men may be instituted into the ministry of acolyte (formerly a step on the path to the priesthood, now a ministry in itself), women and girls may be allowed by the bishop to carry out the liturgical functions of the acolyte, including serving at Mass.

Q Since Catholics observe Sunday as the Lord's day, how can we fulfill our Mass obligation on Saturday afternoon?

A In the early days of the Church, the celebration of great feast days and Sundays began on the vigil—on the evening before the feast or Sunday. This practice continues today. In the Liturgy of the Hours, Saturday evening prayer is called First Evening Prayer of Sunday, or First Vespers of Sunday. So when the Church allowed Sunday Mass on Saturday evening, it was actually going back to an ancient custom. There is a practical reason as well. Many people have to work on Sunday (police, firefighters, medical personnel, and others), and cannot attend Mass. Saturday evening Mass gives them an opportunity to fulfill the Sunday obligation.

Q It is very difficult for me to attend Mass with devotion at our parish. One priest rushes through Mass, and the other speaks with such a heavy accent that it's hard to understand him. Neither is a good preacher. How can I get anything out of Mass under such conditions?

A It is frustrating when you have to deal with language barriers. And it is far worse when priests fail to celebrate the Mass with proper reverence. But even when the priest falls short, Christ is always there. Mother Teresa said that Jesus is found in poor dying lepers of Calcutta "in his most distressing disguise." I disagree. I believe that we priests are Christ's most distressing disguise when we don't celebrate the sacraments with all our heart and soul. But even then, Jesus supplies for our deficiencies. Jesus established his Church in such a way that his grace is bestowed even when the priest is not perfect. Jesus speaks through the Scripture readings. Jesus comes in the love of friends and family at church. Jesus changes bread and wine into himself and enters hearts through holy Communion. It would be better if every priest modeled his words and actions on those of Jesus, but even when the priest fails, Jesus is the same—yesterday, today, and forever (see Heb 13:8). In fact, sometimes people are led to focus on the reality of Christ's presence when the priest is uninspiring. They begin to realize that Christ is the only Savior. Imperfect priests, while they are not the ideal, can actually help us rely more on Christ and less on mere human beings.

Q Are we supposed to fast for an hour before Mass begins, or for an hour before we receive Communion?

A The Church's *Code of Canon Law* states that a person is to abstain for at least one hour before **receiving** holy Communion from any food and drink, except for water and medicine (Canon 919). This regulation, which is quite minimal, provides an opportunity for us to anticipate and prepare for the great privilege of receiving Jesus in holy Communion.

Q I lead singing at our parish, sometimes at two Masses on Sunday. May I receive holy Communion more than once a day?

A Yes, you may. A person who has already received holy Communion may receive it a second time on the same day, but only at a Mass in which the person participates (Canon 917). One should not enter Mass at Communion time just to receive a second time, but should take part in the whole celebration. However, in danger of death a person may receive Communion a second time, even outside Mass (Canon 921 §2).

Q My mother has Alzheimer's disease. She has been a deeply religious person, and taught religious education classes for children years ago. But now she doesn't seem to recognize even family members. Am I obliged to bring her to Mass on Sunday? Is she allowed to receive holy Communion? She is quiet in church and swallows the host as she should, but I suspect she really doesn't know what is happening.

A Trying to decide whether a person with Alzheimer's should receive Communion is difficult. However, only God really knows what is going on at the deepest level of your mother's awareness. But if Mass seems to have a calming effect on her, and if she receives Communion and swallows the host properly, it is certainly permissible to bring her to Mass and have her take Communion. There may be a Person-to-person communication between Jesus and your mother that is a real blessing for her, even if she doesn't understand it completely. The fact that she has been such a faithful Catholic and has taught religious education would be additional reasons for her to receive Communion.

However, I do not think that you are obliged to take her to Mass if this is a hardship. She is excused from any obligation to attend because of her illness. The choice is yours, and you should make that choice realizing that God will respect your decision. You may bring her to church and have her receive Communion, but you do not have an obligation in conscience to do so.

Q Why doesn't the Catholic Church always offer Communion under the forms of bread and wine? On the other hand, if one form is sufficient, why offer both?

A There are two issues involved in receiving holy Communion. The first is the Real Presence of Jesus. The Church believes that the bread and wine are changed into Christ, and that a person who receives either the host or cup receives the whole Christ. When we receive Christ only under the sign of bread, we are receiving the whole Christ. When we receive Christ only under the sign of wine, we are receiving the whole Christ.

The second issue involved is doing what Jesus did at the Last Supper when he gave the apostles, his first priests, Communion under the species of both bread and wine. The Church teaches that the priest must do what the apostles did, receive both species, but that Communion under both kinds is optional for others. At times, it is not possible or advisable to have people drink from the same cup because the numbers at a Mass are so large or because of the danger of disease. Therefore, the Church allows Communion under both kinds in situations where it can be arranged; communicants may then choose whether to receive under both species or not.

Q Doesn't the Catholic Church violate the law against giving liquor to minors when it offers the cup to children?

A This practice is not a violation of civil law, because civil law allows it for religious purposes when parental consent is given.

Q Why can't non-Catholics receive Communion at weddings, funerals, and other celebrations of Mass?

A The Catholic Church has always regarded Communion as a sign that the recipient accepts the teaching of the Church and is a full member of the Church. Justin Martyr, for example, wrote in A.D. 150: "No one may share the Eucharist with us unless he believes that what we teach is true...and unless he lives in accordance with the principles given us by Christ."

However, the Catholic Church does allow baptized non-Catholic Christians to receive holy Communion, the sacrament of the anointing of the sick, and sacrament of penance in danger of death or a grave and pressing need. The *Directory for the Application of Principles and Norms on Ecumenism* (paragraphs 130–131) lists four conditions for reception of the sacrament by baptized non-Catholic Christians in these circumstances. They must be unable to have recourse to a minister of their own church or ecclesial community, ask for the sacrament of their own initiative, manifest Catholic faith in this sacrament, and be properly disposed.

In general, bishops in the United States have interpreted the guidelines to apply to the reception of Communion as follows: Baptized non-Catholics who believe in the Real Presence, and meet the other conditions just listed, can receive holy Communion in danger of death and in serious need (for example, persecution, prison) when they do not have access to their own church community.

The *Directory for the Application of Principles and Norms on Ecumenism* (paragraph 132) also states that Catholics are not permitted to receive communion in Protestant and other churches without a valid priesthood. To do so would imply a unity of belief that does not exist, and an acceptance of communion as a mere symbol of Christ rather than his Real Presence.

Q Jesus never turned away a believer. Why doesn't the Catholic Church welcome everyone and allow all people to receive holy Communion?

A It is true that Jesus did not "turn away any believer." But he did not accept as followers those who chose to believe only what they wanted. In John 6, we see that Jesus expected people to believe exactly what he said, no matter how hard it was. When many would not accept the full truth of what he said, he let them leave. He would not "water down" his teaching about the Eucharist. Jesus was firm in requiring adherence to the truth as he taught it. He upheld the sanctity and permanence of marriage to people who believed in easy divorce (see Mk 10:1–12). He proclaimed the reality of eternal life, and faced down those who thought the belief unsophisticated and naive (see Mk 12:18–27). Jesus denounced people who refused to believe (see Mt 11:20–24) and those who hardened their hearts against him (see Mt 23). He expected his followers to have standards for membership in the

Church, and he stated that those who violated them were to be excluded: "...if the offender refuses to listen even to the church, let such a one be to you as a Gentile and a tax collector" (Mt 18:17).

This may sound harsh, but Jesus did not take the truth lightly. Jesus expected the Church to safeguard the truth. When the Church says that communicants must accept the full truth of Christ regarding the Eucharist as the Church teaches that truth, it is being faithful to Christ.

There is some discussion today about how the conditions for administering Communion to non-Catholics should be interpreted. But we must be aware that problems exist, and we must not make light of them. Catholics who cooperate in abortions would commit a grave sin of sacrilege if they received holy Communion without repenting. Should non-Catholic abortionists be allowed to receive holy Communion if they claim to be in "good conscience" and to meet the conditions for receiving Communion? Of course not.

Doctrinal differences and moral standards are important. The Church cannot abandon its belief in the sacraments or its pro-life commitments. Any discussion of intercommunion that ignores such issues will end in confusion. The road to full unity will be long and difficult, but it is a road that must be walked with courage, fidelity to the truth, and charity. Jesus himself would expect no less.

Finally, in a very real sense, the Catholic Church does not turn away any believer. It says: "This is what we believe. If you choose to believe this and become one of us, a member of this family of believers, then you are invited to share in our family meal, the Eucharist. If you choose not to accept our beliefs, we respect yours, even if we do not agree with them. We respect your right to share in your family meal, but we ask that you respect our beliefs about our own family meal."

Q A coworker claims that if we Catholics really believe we eat the Body and Blood of Christ we are guilty of cannibalism. How do I respond to him?

A We should note that people who level this charge against Catholics place themselves in bad company. The pagans attacked the first Christians by accusing them of cannibalism. Early Church writers like Tertullian had to refute such challenges. This proves two things. One, a belief in Christ's Real Presence existed in the early Church, because a simple "memorial supper" would not have drawn such slander from the pagans. Two, those who today attack Catholics for "cannibalism" align themselves with the pagans of early Christian times! From another viewpoint, people who attack Catholics for believing in the Real Presence must explain away passages such as John 6:53: "Very truly, I tell you, unless you eat the flesh of the Son of Man and drink his blood, you have no life in you." Jesus asks us to eat his flesh and drink his blood." As was explained in Chapter Five (p. 94), for the Jewish people "flesh" or "body" was the person, and "blood" was life, so Jesus was saying that we must receive him. But this is not cannibalism. Cannibalism refers to the act of killing other human beings and eating them so that their flesh and blood are absorbed into those who eat them. Christ is not killed when received in Communion because his body is glorified. Christ is not absorbed into us at Communion, but united to us, and we are united with him. Jesus says in John 6:56: "Those who eat my flesh and drink my blood abide in me, and I in them."

Q How can I get more out of the Mass? How can I make the Mass more meaningful in my everyday life?

A I wrote the first five chapters to help answer the first question. The final chapter answers the second. Working on this book has certainly helped me reflect on answers to both questions!

QUESTIONS FOR
DISCUSSION AND REFLECTION

Which questions in this chapter have you asked or wondered about? How would you improve the answers given to the questions? Do you disagree with any of the answers in the chapter? If so, what would your answers be? What other questions do you have about the Mass?

ACTIVITIES

Consider this sentence from the first paragraph of this chapter: "Often the best answer to a question about the Mass is personal witness, and any answer can be enhanced by the sharing of one's own experience." Study each of the questions, and consider how you might relate your own personal experience to each answer.

Ask the Holy Spirit to open your mind and heart to the full meaning of the Mass, and to help you respond with charity and wisdom to any questions you might be asked about the Eucharist.

Chapter Seven

EUCHARISTIC
SPIRITUALITY

⸙

A n Irish bishop recited the following ditty during a sermon:
"Paddy Murphy went to Mass, and never missed a Sunday.
But Paddy Murphy went to hell, for what he did on Monday."

There's an important lesson in this ditty, that our lives must
be in conformity with our worship. The name Mass, as we have
seen, comes from the Latin dismissal formula, "Ite, Missa est."

The Eucharist, the *Catechism of the Catholic Church* adds,
is called "*Holy Mass (Missa)*, because the liturgy in which the
mystery of salvation is accomplished concludes with the sending
forth *(missio)* of the faithful, so that they may fulfill God's will
in their daily lives" (CCC 1332).

"Go in peace, glorifying the Lord by your life," we leave
the church building after Mass to go and live the Mass. This is
"Eucharistic Spirituality."

LIVING THE MASS

The word *spirituality* has many meanings. To understand its most
profound sense, however, we should begin with the Mass as it is
described in this passage from the *Catechism*:

The Eucharist is "the source and summit of the Christian life" (Lumen Gentium). *"The other sacraments, and indeed all ecclesiastical ministries and works of the apostolate, are bound up with the Eucharist and are oriented toward it. For in the blessed Eucharist is contained the whole spiritual good of the Church, namely Christ himself, our Pasch"* (Presbyterorum ordinis, 5) *(CCC 1324).*

Spirituality is the spiritual life, that is, living in God, with God, and for God. Spirituality begins with the realization that our world of material things does not mark out the boundaries of our existence. The "really real," with no beginning or end, is God, who is being itself: "I AM WHO I AM" (Ex 3:14). To the extent that we share in God's life and are united to the love of Father, Son, and Holy Spirit, our life expands beyond the limits of space and time. It shakes off the shackles imposed by weakness or age. It reaches to horizons that never end because they shine with God's everlasting light.

Some humans tend to live as if physical matter were the only reality. This misconception is reinforced by advertising which, for obvious reasons, focuses on what can be bought and sold. The material world is real, and it is good. It bears the stamp of divine approval. "God saw everything that he had made, and indeed, it was very good" (Gen 1:31). But it is limited. The goodness of material things and of human bodily existence flows from its source, unlimited Goodness, almighty God. Matter is created by the divine wisdom and energy which gave it being. After all, as Einstein demonstrated, $E = mc^2$!

True spirituality recognizes God's presence in all creation. Created things are not God, of course, but they point to God as their maker and sustainer: "The heavens are telling the glory of God" (Ps 19:1). Sin placed a veil between humanity and God's glory, as the story of creation shows so dramatically in the attempt of Adam and Eve to hide from God (see Gen 3:8). But Jesus Christ removed that veil when he came into our world. At his birth, the glory of the Lord shone upon the humblest of people (see Lk 2:9). When lowly shepherds looked upon Jesus, they saw "the glory of God in the face of Jesus Christ" (2 Cor 4:6). Catholic spirituality, then, *is* Jesus Christ.

LIVING IS CHRIST

For this, we have no less an authority than Saint Paul. "For to me," he wrote, "living is Christ..." (Phil 1:21). To be a Catholic, to live a Catholic spiritual life, is to know Christ as Son of God and as our Lord and Savior. The *Catechism of the Catholic Church* states:

> *"At the heart of catechesis we find, in essence, a Person, the Person of Jesus of Nazareth, the only Son from the Father...who suffered and died for us and who now, after rising, is living with us forever." To catechize is "to reveal in the Person of Christ the whole of God's eternal design reaching fulfillment in that Person. It is to seek to understand the meaning of Christ's actions and words and of the signs worked by him." Catechesis aims at putting "people...in communion...with Jesus Christ: only he can lead us to the love of the Father in the Spirit and make us share in the life of the Holy Trinity" (CCC 426, quoting* Catechesi tradendae, *5).*

How does the Mass fit into this statement? Jesus alone can bestow true spirituality by granting us a share in the life of the Holy Trinity. God comes to us in Jesus Christ. And Jesus comes to us first and foremost in the Mass. As we stated in Chapter One:

God "condenses" divinity in Jesus to reveal the incredible extent of divine love in the heart of God. Then Jesus "condenses" the power of his life, death, and Resurrection in the Mass; he "condenses" his humanity and divinity in the Eucharist. Through the Mass and in holy Communion, we meet God!

That is why the Eucharist is the "source and summit of the Christian life," for "in the blessed Eucharist is contained...Christ himself." We who are Catholic must be sure of this. Our beliefs, sacraments, apostolic works, ministries, lives, and spirituality are centered in Christ.

Sadly, some Catholics fail to realize this point. A few years ago Miriam told me that she never knew Jesus while she was a Catholic. The day after Pope John Paul II visited Saint Louis, a caller to a radio talk show announced that he didn't know Jesus personally until he left Catholicism. Obviously, such people could not have understood their Catholic Faith, or believed what the Church teaches. They could not have recognized Christ's Real Presence in the Eucharist and in his Church. But how could they miss it?

When I asked this question during a discussion at a religious education convention, one teacher said she thought the reason might be that "Catholicism has so many riches to present that we forget to relate them to Jesus." But the *Catechism* tells us: "In catechesis 'Christ, the Incarnate Word and Son of God...is taught—everything else is taught with reference to him'" (CCC 427, quoting *Catechesi tradendae*, 5). We must relate all the riches of our faith to Jesus, find Jesus in them, and bring to the world these riches—above all—the riches of the Eucharist.

"Either/Or, Both/And"

If some Catholics fail to find Jesus in the Catholic Church, those outside the Church who criticize Catholicism surely do not understand how Jesus makes himself available. After Pope John Paul II celebrated Mass at the America's Center in Saint Louis on January 27, 1999, those of us who attended were approached by people handing out anti-Catholic brochures attacking various aspects of Catholic belief. One pamphlet read: "Friend, you can RIGHT NOW be saved and KNOW that you have ETERNAL LIFE, if you will put your complete faith in Jesus Christ, and stop relying on yourself, church, sacraments, or anything else to save or help save you. Jesus is the Savior. Do you believe he can save you, or don't you?"

Those who compose such anti-Catholic literature separate Christ from the Church he founded and deny his teachings. The Church did not create the sacraments. Jesus did. It was Jesus who said: "This is my Body" and "If you forgive the sins of others, they are forgiven."

Unfortunately, those who attack Catholicism often rely on false "either-or" dilemmas. "Do you believe in Jesus, *or* do you believe in his church and sacraments?" We Catholics believe that Christianity is a matter, not of "either/or," but of "both/and." We believe in Jesus Christ *and* in his Church and sacraments. It is through the Church and sacraments that Jesus comes to us today. Jesus is not only a historical figure. Jesus is not just up in the sky. He's right here with us, through the Church and sacraments which make his presence both visible and tangible.

Catholicism is a sacramental Church. We believe that God the Son became one of us so that he might be a visible sign (*sacrament*) of God's presence. The seven sacraments given us by Jesus Christ are the visible signs through which he continues to act in our midst. The Eucharist **is** Jesus, and therefore the source and summit of sacramental life, as the *Catechism* states. "The other sacraments...are bound up with the Eucharist and are oriented toward it" (CCC 1324, quoting *Presbyterorum ordinis*, 5).

The more we know about the Eucharist, the more we will be brought to Jesus. After all, it is Jesus who leads us in prayer at Mass, who proclaims the Scriptures to us, and who makes his dwelling in our hearts at holy Communion. And it is Jesus whom we can proclaim to those who, perhaps out of misguided zeal, ask questions, such as "Have you accepted Jesus as your savior?" "Are you saved?" Our response to the first question might be: "Yes, I accept Jesus into my heart each time I receive him in holy Communion. He abides in me and I abide in him" (see Jn 6:56). Our answer to the second: "Jesus died for my salvation, and he makes the power of his death and Resurrection present to me at every Mass. I set all my hope on the grace that Jesus brings (see 1 Pet 1:13). Salvation is my life's journey."

When confronted by such questions, we should always explain our reason for hope, as Scripture says, "with gentleness and reverence" (1 Pet 3:16), and even with a sense of humor. Jerry was playing tennis when he fell backward on the concrete court, fracturing his skull in three places. His friends called 911, and a helicopter quickly landed nearby. A paramedic stabilized him and kept him alive while he was flown to a hospital. Later Jerry met the paramedic. He was Hispanic, and his name was Jesus. Jerry smiles and says, "I feel blessed to have been saved by Jesus!"

We have all been saved by Jesus in the sense that through his life, death, and Resurrection Jesus has done everything necessary to bring us to heaven. But we must, in our turn, freely stay united to Jesus by faith and good works (see Jas 2:26; Eph 2:10). Salvation *is* our life's journey!

FATHER, SON, AND HOLY SPIRIT

If we meet Jesus at every Mass and realize how he is the heart and center of our Catholic faith, we cannot help but be led into a deeper relationship with the Father and Holy Spirit as well. In Chapter Four (p. 78), we saw how Christ stretched out his arms on the cross to unite us to himself, to the Father, and to the Holy Spirit. We saw how in his Last Supper discourse (see Jn 13–17), Jesus promised that he, the Father, and the Holy Spirit would live in us. Jesus wanted us to see the Mass as a means of joining ourselves to the life and love of the Trinity.

For we live in a Trinitarian world. From all eternity the Father knows himself with a knowledge so perfect that it is a person, the Son. The Father and Son love each other with a love so perfect that it is a person, the Holy Spirit. From this knowledge and love flow all created things and persons, including ourselves. Since we have been made by God, who is perfect knowledge and love, we hunger for perfect truth and love. That hunger will be satisfied only to the extent that we know and love God as Father, Son, and Holy Spirit. Mass is the best opportunity this side of heaven to strengthen our relationship with Father, Son, and Spirit.

Every Mass brings us into contact with the Trinity. As Mass begins, we make the Sign of the Cross. As Mass ends, Father, Son, and Holy Spirit bless us. During Mass, we pray to the Father, through Jesus Christ our Lord, in the unity of the Holy Spirit. We profess our Faith in Father, Son, and Holy Spirit. At Mass, Jesus offers a perfect sacrifice of love to the Father, and we are privileged to join our own love to his. The Holy Spirit helps us make our offering and pray as we ought. When we receive Jesus in holy Communion, we receive also the Father and Holy Spirit, who are one with him.

Each time we leave Mass, going in peace to glorify God by our lives, Jesus invites us to live a Trinitarian spirituality. In my book *The Search for Happiness,* I explain an approach to this spirituality built around the Lord's Prayer, the beatitudes, and the fruits of the Holy Spirit. Here I would like to suggest a three-minute prayer to help anyone stay in touch with the Trinity. In the first minute, think about the greatest blessing you've received in the past twenty-four hours and thank God the Father for that blessing. In the second, consider your most significant failing in the past twenty-four hours and ask Jesus to forgive you. In the third, look ahead to the greatest challenge that faces you in the next twenty-four hours and ask the Holy Spirit to be your helper and guide as you accept that challenge. Use this prayer often, and you'll be more conscious of the reality that we are "the temple of the living God" (2 Cor 6:16).

LIVING THE PASCHAL MYSTERY

The Mass, as we saw in Chapter Two (p. 29), commemorates and makes present the Paschal Mystery, Christ's work of re-demption brought about primarily by his passion, death, Res-urrection, and Ascension (CCC 1067; see also the *Catechism Glossary).* Christ's Passover from death to life, his passage from death on the cross to glory at the Father's right hand, is presented at every Mass so that we might praise and thank God for this great act of love. The Paschal Mystery is presented also as a pattern for us. With Christ we conquer death and rise to new life. "Save us, Savior of the world, for by your Cross and Resurrection you have set us free." In Christ our greatest fears are overcome as death is defeated and we learn to live in the freedom of God's children.

The Paschal Mystery shines light into every darkness. There is a kind of death in many of life's trials: the frustration of failure, the loss of a job, misunderstandings in the family, the departure of a friend, the onset of illness, the pain of depression, the betrayal of a trust. Such deaths weigh us down and drain us of energy and hope.

To these deaths the Paschal Mystery brings resurrection. At Calvary, Christ's mission seemed to have failed utterly. His disciples despaired. But Easter bestowed life where there had been death. Jesus brings hope into every situation. He is, as he declared at the Last Supper, "the way, and the truth, and the life" (Jn 14:6).

His death and Resurrection are the *way* through every hard journey we face. His teaching in Scripture, proclaimed at every Mass, is the *truth* that guides us in times of confusion and failure. His Real Presence in holy Communion is the *life* that lifts us from any grave of discouragement or fear.

As Jesus walked with the two disciples on the way to Emmaus, so he wants to walk with us every day. We need not leave him in church! As Jesus speaks to us in the readings at Mass, so he wants to speak to us each time we read the Bible. The Scriptures are not confined to the pulpit! As Jesus gives us his life in holy Communion, so he desires to abide in us always, allowing the life of his grace to flow through our veins. We the branches are not separated from Christ the Vine when we exit Mass for home!

THE LITURGICAL YEAR

People like to celebrate birthdays and anniversaries. We have holidays to recall milestones in our nation's history. Such celebrations help us remember the past. They bring joy and festivity. They refresh and invigorate us for the routine of everyday existence. The liturgical year is the Church's way of celebrating and reliving the great events of salvation. Each year follows a pattern, and the readings and prayers for Mass have been organized to bring joy and festivity, refreshment and new vigor to the ever-changing seasons of life.

The liturgical year begins with Advent, four weeks of preparation for Christmas. On December 25 we observe the birthday of Christ and reflect on the Incarnation. After Christmas other feasts extend the celebration: Holy Family Sunday, the Solemnity of Mary the Mother of God (New Year's Day), Epiphany, and the Baptism of the Lord.

There follows a period of Ordinary Time, the length of which depends on the date of Easter. The Lenten preparation for Easter begins on Ash Wednesday, when we are marked with ashes signaling our desire to make the Paschal Mystery the pattern of our existence. As catechumens make final preparations for baptism, all Catholics are challenged to die to sin and rise to new life. Lent ends at the sacred triduum, three days which recall the events of the first Holy Thursday, Good Friday, and Holy Saturday. We celebrate the Resurrection with the Easter Vigil and the Masses of Easter, the greatest feast of the Church year. Easter season continues through the Feast of the Ascension and ends on Pentecost Sunday.

Ordinary Time resumes the day after Pentecost, but the next two Sundays commemorate the Trinity and the Body and Blood of Christ. Ordinary Time continues through the last Sunday of the liturgical year, the Solemnity of Christ the King, after which the First Sunday of Advent starts the cycle again.

Christ is free of the limits of space and time, and relives with us the events of his life through the liturgical year. Through Scripture readings appropriate to the events being celebrated, God speaks to us. We respond by participating in the liturgy, and so are joined to the birth, life, dying, and rising of Jesus, as once again he walks the pathways of our world.

Most major liturgical observances occur on Sunday, but there are also special feasts in the liturgical year called holy days of obligation. In the United States we observe the following holy days: Christmas on the twenty-fifth of December; the Solemnity of Mary the Mother of God on the first of January; Ascension (now usually celebrated on the Seventh Sunday of Easter); Mary's Assumption on the fifteenth of August; All Saints' Day on the first of November; and the Immaculate Conception on the eighth of December.

Throughout the liturgical year the Catholic Church keeps feast days in honor of Mary and the saints. As we remember their lives in special prayers at Mass and ask them to pray for us, we heed the biblical command: "Remember your leaders, those who spoke the word of God to you; consider the outcome of their way of life, and imitate their faith" (Heb 13:7). Commemorating the saints also proclaims the centrality of Christ, for their lives demonstrate the power of his life, death, and Resurrection shared with humanity. The saints show the joy and beauty of putting Jesus first and letting his Paschal Mystery be the pattern for our lives.

THE OTHER SACRAMENTS

"The other sacraments...are bound up with the Eucharist and are oriented toward it" (CCC 1324). It is Jesus who is present in the Eucharist, and it is Jesus who speaks and acts through all the sacraments. The Mass makes present the Paschal Mystery of Jesus' life, death, Resurrection, and Ascension, and the other sacraments also give us a share in this Mystery. The Church professes belief in these realities and in the interconnection between the Mass and sacraments in many ways. Here we will note how the celebration of the Eucharist is linked to that of the other sacraments.

Baptism, which first joins us to Christ in his dying and rising, is most dramatically united to the Eucharist in the great Easter Vigil which welcomes new members into the Church. As the congregation is drawn from the darkness of night into the light of Christ, the baptized step from the darkness of sin into the brightness of God's grace. They receive an outpouring of the

Holy Spirit in confirmation, then are nourished with the Body and Blood of Jesus.

Ritual Masses for confirmation, holy orders, matrimony, and the anointing of the sick highlight the eucharistic presence and power of Jesus. In confirmation, he pours out the Holy Spirit, a gift made possible by his passion, death, and Resurrection (see Jn 16:7). In holy orders, Jesus says to the newly ordained what he said to the apostles at the Last Supper: "Do this in memory of me." In matrimony, Jesus, living in the bride and groom, binds them together in their exchange of vows and in their acceptance of his Body and Blood; their love then becomes a sign of his love for the Church (see Eph 5:32). In the anointing of the sick, Jesus offers the healing power of the love he demonstrated by his death, and he gives comfort and hope as those anointed receive him in Communion.

The penitential rite at Mass reminds us that we are sinners in need of God's forgiveness. It assures us, as we pray "Lord, have mercy," that the same Jesus who gathers us together at the Eucharist is ever present in the sacrament of penance to forgive our sins.

Finally, when life on this earth has ended for believers, the funeral Mass proclaims that those who die with Christ rise with him to eternal life. Jesus speaks words of consolation to the bereaved in the Scripture readings. He unites them to their loved one in the Eucharistic Prayer. He promises them at Communion that those who eat this bread will live forever (see Jn 6:58).

From birth until death, from baptism through the anointing of the sick and funeral Mass, we are reassured by eucharistic celebrations that Jesus continues to share with us the love and grace he lavished upon the apostles at the Last Supper. Indeed, "the other sacraments...are bound up with the Eucharist and are oriented toward it."

EUCHARISTIC DEVOTIONS

In every parish I've served as a priest, I have been blessed by the dedication of people who attend daily Mass. Physicians, business owners, teachers, and laborers rise early to worship at Mass before dawn. Home-schooling moms bring their children to the Eucharist before starting classes. Retirees begin their day with prayer and the Mass. Some folks cannot come every day but attend whenever possible. Such individuals radiate faith in Jesus and love of others by the sacrifices they make in uniting themselves to the sacrifice of the Mass. They have inspired me, and they have been avenues of God's grace for countless others.

Daily Mass is *the* most powerful way to live a eucharistic spirituality. The Sunday Mass, as we have seen, has a special place in the Church's liturgy. It is the Lord's day. But every day belongs to God, and there is no better way to let Jesus touch our lives than union with him at daily Mass.

However, it is not possible for many people to attend Mass every day. For such individuals there are other eucharistic devotions to help them stay close to Jesus. Christ's Real Presence in the Eucharist remains after Mass is over. For this reason, the Catholic Church preserves the Blessed Sacrament in tabernacles throughout the world to make Communion available to the sick and to allow the faithful to adore Christ in the Eucharist.

The Church highly recommends public and private devotion to the holy Eucharist outside Mass. An important public devotion is exposition of the Blessed Sacrament with Benediction, an act of liturgical worship. The consecrated host is placed on the altar in a monstrance (a sacred vessel in which the host may be seen). Scriptures are read, prayers are said, hymns are sung, and some time is devoted to silent prayer. Adoration may be expressed by the use of incense. Then the congregation is blessed with the Holy Sacrament, and the service concludes with prayers and a hymn. This devotion, of course, is a clear demonstration of our Catholic belief in Christ's Eucharistic Presence, and it nourishes and strengthens that belief.

Pope John Paul II emphasized the value of eucharistic adoration, the practice of spending time with Jesus in the Blessed Sacrament. In his encyclical letter *Ecclesia De Eucharistia*, he points out both the importance of this devotion and its relationship to the Mass:

The worship of the Eucharist outside of the Mass is of inestimable value for the life of the Church. This worship is strictly linked to the celebration of the Eucharistic Sacrifice. The presence of Christ under the sacred species reserved after Mass—a presence which lasts as long as the species of bread and of wine remain—derives from the celebration of the sacrifice and is directed towards communion, both sacramental and spiritual (25).

Many Catholic parishes have instituted the practice of perpetual adoration, where members of the faithful maintain a constant presence before the Blessed Sacrament exposed on the altar. Other parishes set aside a day or two each week for adoration. From such eucharistic adoration flow many benefits, including vocations to the priesthood and religious life, new appreciation of the sacrament of matrimony, and greater concern for charity and justice.

Whether the Blessed Sacrament is exposed or not, Jesus remains available to us in every Catholic church. An hour in the presence of Jesus has been a source of grace for many. Bishop Fulton Sheen, in his retreat talks, strongly recommended the practice of spending an hour every day in the presence of the Blessed Sacrament. This hour has been for me one of the greatest blessings of my priesthood. I heartily recommend it to all. If you can't fit in an hour every day, try an hour a week. It will make the rest of your week more pleasant and productive.

What might we do during this hour of prayer? First, there should be time to enjoy being with Jesus, as did Andrew and another apostle who met Jesus and spent a day visiting with him (Jn 1:35–42). They must have talked about their families, their work, and what was happening in their lives. So too can we. We can receive, as the pope suggests, "spiritual communion"—inviting Jesus to live in our hearts even when we cannot receive him sacramentally. We may pray the rosary, paying special attention to how the mysteries relate to the Eucharist, to the presence of Jesus, to his teaching, and to the Paschal Mystery of his passion, death, Resurrection, and Ascension. We should reflect upon Scripture, especially those passages used at the Sunday Masses, another excellent way to relate our time of adoration to the Mass. Some individuals like to read from a good Catholic book, pausing to talk to Jesus about thoughts that touch their hearts. Those who get into the habit of making an hour of adoration in the presence of Jesus find that the time goes by all too quickly, just as it does in the presence of any good friend!

As we develop our awareness of Christ's Real Presence in all the tabernacles of the world, we learn to notice Catholic churches and to say a prayer to Jesus as we walk or drive past his home. We pray a "morning offering" early in the day, giving to the Father our hopes, plans, and efforts in union with the offering of Jesus in Masses being celebrated at that moment. We make a spiritual Communion anytime or anywhere, remembering Jesus' words: "Listen! I am standing at the door, knocking; if you hear my voice and open the door, I will come in to you and eat with you, and you with me" (Rev 3:20).

Pope John Paul II, in his apostolic letter *Dies Domini,* refers to televised Masses as a means of joining oneself to the Eucharist. Televised Masses do not take the place of Sunday Mass, but as the pope notes:

...for those who cannot take part in the Eucharist and who are therefore excused from the obligation, radio and television are a precious help, especially if accompanied by the generous service of extraordinary ministers who bring the Eucharist to the sick, also bringing them the greeting and solidarity of the whole community. Sunday Mass thus produces rich fruits for these Christians too, and they are truly enabled to experience Sunday as "the Lord's Day" and "the Church's day" (54).

Televised Masses allow anyone to grow in love of the Eucharist, as they provide a pattern for prayer and reflection. Special Masses, such as those celebrated by the Holy Father and shown worldwide, help us appreciate the power of the Eucharist to touch all people and to draw us together in Christ.

The pope's mention of extraordinary ministers who bring Communion to the sick highlights another element of eucharistic spirituality that is a great blessing for ministers and for the homebound. It is a blessing to hold Jesus close to one's heart, to talk with him on the way, to share the grace of his presence with those who otherwise could not receive him. It is a blessing for the sick and elderly to have Jesus enter their residence, to light up their lives, to be one with them in their suffering, to lessen their pain, and to assure them that he will be with them forever.

THE EUCHARIST AND LOVING SERVICE

At the Last Supper, Jesus forged an unbreakable bond between works of charity and the Eucharist. He washed the feet of the apostles, then said, "For I have set you an example, that you also should do as I have done to you" (Jn 13:15). Later that evening Jesus remarked: "This is my commandment, that you love one another as I have loved you" (Jn 15:12).

From New Testament times, followers of Jesus have attended to his words and example. In the Acts of the Apostles, the believers "devoted themselves to the apostles' teaching and fellowship, to the breaking of bread and the prayers" (Acts 2:42). The same ones who met for the breaking of the bread "would sell their possessions and goods and distribute the proceeds to all, as any had need" (Acts 2:45).

Saint Paul, writing to the Corinthians about a collection for the poor in Jerusalem, linked this work of charity to the Sunday Eucharist, repeating directions he had given also to the churches of Galatia. "On the first day of every week, each of you is to put aside and save whatever extra you earn..." (1 Cor 16:2). Earlier in his letter, because the Corinthians had neglected the bond between the Eucharist and concern for the poor, Paul sternly rebuked them: "When you come together, it is not really to eat the Lord's supper. For when the time comes to eat, each of you goes ahead with your own supper, and one goes hungry and another becomes drunk. What! Do you not have homes to eat and drink in? Or do you show contempt for the church of God and humiliate those who have nothing?" (1 Cor 11:20–22).

Saint Justin Martyr demonstrates that the next generation of Christians learned the lessons taught by Paul. After describing the Sunday celebration of the Eucharist (passage cited in Chapter Two, p. 36), he states:

*And they who are well to do, and willing, give what each thinks fit; and what is collected is deposited with the president, who helps the orphans and widows and those who, through sickness or any other cause, are in want, and those who are in bonds and the strangers sojourning among us, and in a word takes care of all who are in need (*First Apology, Chapter 67, *available at catholic-forum. com/saints/stj29002.htm, accessed January 12, 2011).*

Pope John Paul II affirms that the Sunday Eucharist commits Catholics to the works of charity, mercy, and apostolic outreach:

From the Sunday Mass there flows a tide of charity destined to spread into the whole life of the faithful....They look around to find people who may need their help. It may be that in their neighborhood or among those they know there are sick people, elderly people, children or immigrants who precisely on Sundays feel more keenly their isolation, needs and suffering....Inviting to a meal people who are alone, visiting the sick, providing food for needy families, spending a few hours in voluntary work and acts of solidarity: these would certainly be ways of bringing into people's lives the love of Christ received at the Eucharistic table (Dies Domini, 72).

In his encyclical letter *Ecclesia de Eucharistia* the pope speaks of how the Mass gives hope and spurs us on to address the urgent needs of our time, to work for peace, justice, solidarity, and respect for human life. Inherent in the Eucharist is a "commitment to transforming the world in accordance with the Gospel" (#20). Jesus himself teaches that our eternal salvation depends on personal efforts to serve him in others. "Come, you that are blessed by my Father, inherit the kingdom prepared for you from the foundation of the world; for I was hungry and you gave me food, I was thirsty and you gave me something to drink, I was a stranger and you welcomed me" (Mt 25:34–35). The *Catechism of the Catholic Church* says simply, "The Eucharist commits us to the poor" (CCC 1397).

CHARITY BEGINS AT HOME

At the Last Supper Jesus washed the feet of his apostles, who were his chosen family. Charity does begin at home, and our works of charity and justice should start among those with whom we live. It is often easier to show kindness and patience to strangers than to family members, whose failings are obvious and ever present.

It can be easier to dream of saving the world than to love the ones you're with. At times we all feel like the little boy who said, "I know Jesus loves everyone, but he never met my sister." Well, Jesus' apostles were far from perfect, and he loved them anyway. We, too, must love our family members anyway, striving to focus on their good points and to forgive their weaknesses.

At Mass we listen to God's Word to learn how to love. We are joined to the love and sacrificial giving of Jesus. We receive him in holy Communion. We must bring him home with us. I often ask children, "If Jesus would disguise himself as you, and then went home instead of you, would your family notice a difference?" Their response is always in the affirmative, and always with a smile. Then I'll suggest: "Why don't you pretend you are Jesus. Try to think, talk, and act like him. Surprise your family!"

This would be good advice for any of us. If we think like Jesus, we will look for the best in others. We will subdue thoughts of anger and feelings of resentment. We will consider the needs of others before our own. If we speak like Jesus, we will use words of encouragement rather than of criticism, words of forgiveness rather than of hostility, words of respect rather than of sarcasm, words of gratitude rather than of complaint. If we act like Jesus, we will express love in practical ways, performing everyday tasks for others when no one but God will notice, being polite, considerate, and thoughtful. The sacramental presence of Jesus ceases when the sacramental species no longer exist. But Jesus continues to live in us when our thoughts, words, and deeds mirror his love and goodness.

Receiving the Bread of Life, the disciples of Christ ready themselves to undertake with the strength of the Risen Lord and his Spirit the tasks which await them in their ordinary life. For the faithful who have understood the meaning of what they have done, the eucharistic celebration does not stop at the church door. Like the first witnesses of the Resurrection, Christians who gather each Sunday to experience and proclaim the presence of the Risen Lord are called to evangelize and bear witness in their daily lives (John Paul II, Dies Domini, *45).*

WHAT THEY DID ON MONDAY

The Eucharist is surely "the source and summit of the Christian life." Eucharistic spirituality is knowing Jesus Christ as our way, truth, and life. It is entering, through Jesus, into the life of the Trinity. It is living the Paschal Mystery, knowing that Jesus will transform our suffering and death into resurrection and new life. It is walking with Jesus through the liturgical year, allowing the events of his life to be a pattern for ours. It is union with Jesus through prayer, eucharistic adoration, and attentiveness to his presence. It is serving the cause of justice and charity. It is taking Jesus home as we "go and announce the Gospel of the Lord."

Living a eucharistic spirituality will make it possible for us one day to hear the words of a new ditty:

"These Catholics went to Mass and never missed a Sunday. And these Catholics went to HEAVEN for what they did on Monday!"

QUESTIONS FOR
DISCUSSION AND REFLECTION

Can you give your own definition of spirituality? Of Christian spirituality? Is it possible to live a truly Christian spirituality without being religious, without participating in religious rites? What do you think of the response given on page 15 to those who say, "I'm spiritual, but not religious"?

When asked why he goes to daily Mass and what it has meant to him, Jim responded: "Going to daily Mass helps me to remember to put God first in my life, to give God glory, and to get to know God better. I have a sense of peace in my life even in the midst of very difficult situations. Mass has also helped lead me back to frequent confession, which has also been an incredible blessing. Daily Mass has strengthened my family life." If you attend daily Mass, what does it mean to you? If not, what could it mean for you if you did?

There are many suggestions in this chapter for living a eucharistic spirituality. First scan the main headings of this chapter. Then consider: What additional aspects of eucharistic spirituality do you think should be discussed within these headings? What other headings do you think should be added? Are there approaches to spirituality in this chapter with which you disagree? Why? (Any criticisms, comments, or suggestions may be sent to the author at frlukecm@cs.com.)

ACTIVITIES

Christian spirituality is the spiritual life, living in God, with God, and for God, with Jesus as our guide and model. It includes much more than can be included in this chapter. For an explanation of how living in Christ finds expression in Catholic moral teaching, see Chapter Fourteen of my book *"We Believe..." A Survey of the*

Catholic Faith (Liguori Publications, 1995). As already noted, *The Search for Happiness* (Liguori, 2002) offers an outline for living a Trinitarian spirituality built on the Lord's Prayer, the beatitudes, and the fruits of the Holy Spirit. *The Privilege of Being Catholic* (Liguori, 1993) shows that our Catholic Faith and spirituality are sacramental in nature because Jesus himself is a visible, sacramental sign of God's reality and presence. And remember that any Catholic spirituality must include the Eucharist precisely because, as the *Catechism of the Catholic Church* states, it is "the source and summit of the Christian life."

Mary stood by the cross of Jesus and shared his suffering. She can help us draw strength from her crucified Son at every Mass and in every place. A Marian devotion I've found very helpful is to replace feelings of anger and frustration with a "Hail Mary" for those who test my patience. On some days I say a lot of "Hail Marys"! But I find that the prayers bring far more peace and happiness than giving in to hostile emotions. I try to remember that Mary, standing at the cross, endured more misunderstanding and hatred in three hours than I will in a lifetime. Mary thereby helps me learn how to live the Mass each day. Try this way of praying and she will help you too.

BIBLIOGRAPHY

Cabié, Robert. *The Eucharist*. Translated by Matthew J. O'Connell. Volume II of *The Church at Prayer, New Edition*. Edited by Aimé Georges Martimort. Collegeville, Minn.: The Liturgical Press, 1986.

Catechism of the Catholic Church. Second Edition. United States Catholic Conference, 1997.

General Instruction of the Roman Missal. United States Catholic Conference, 2010.

Loret, Pierre. *The Story of the Mass*. Liguori, Mo.: Liguori Publications, 1982.

Lukefahr, Oscar. *The Privilege of Being Catholic*. Liguori, Mo.: Liguori Publications, 1993.

_____. *The Search for Happiness*. Liguori, Mo.: Liguori Publications, 2002.

_____. *"We Believe..." A Survey of the Catholic Faith*. Second Edition. Liguori, Mo.: Liguori Publications, 1995.

New Revised Standard Version of the Bible: Catholic Edition. Nashville, Tenn.: Catholic Bible Press. 1993.

Ratzinger, Joseph Cardinal. *The Spirit of the Liturgy*. Translated by John Saward. San Francisco, Ca.: Ignatius Press, 2000.

Schroeder, Gerald L. *The Science of God*. New York: The Free Press. 1997.